Live Life Abundantly!

LIVE LIFE ABUNDANTLY!

Begin NOW to Reach Your Lifetime Goals
with 25 Goal-Achieving Techniques

THOMAS A. HARRIS

Copyright © 2012 by Thomas A. Harris.

Library of Congress Control Number: 2012909255
ISBN: Hardcover   978-1-4771-1709-5
               Softcover   978-1-4771-1708-8

All rights reserved. No part of this book may be reproduced or transmitted in any form or by any means, electronic or mechanical, including photocopying, recording, or by any information storage and retrieval system, without permission in writing from the copyright owner.

This book was printed in the United States of America.

To order additional copies of this book, contact:
Xlibris Corporation
1-888-795-4274
www.Xlibris.com
Orders@Xlibris.com
46380

Contents

Acknowledgments 7
Introduction 9

Chapter 1 Why Should I Set Goals? 13
Chapter 2 What Goals Should I Set? 22
Chapter 3 The Goal-Setting Process 36
Chapter 4 The Four Stages of Goal Achievement 47
Chapter 5 Planning and Mental Stage: Plan It! 51
Chapter 6 Action Stage: Making It Happen! 60
Chapter 7 Persistence Stage: Sticking to It! 67
Chapter 8 Achievement Stage: Achieving It! 81
Chapter 9 Planting Seeds for Lifetime Achievement 91

Conclusion 97
About the Author 101
Appendix 105

Life is but a series of goals. Some small ones, some big, some mundane and some audacious! Success happens when we pick the right ones to attempt, we enjoy the pursuit and we even achieve some of them!

Thomas Harris

Acknowledgments

First and above all, I would like to thank God for continuing to push, pull, and guide me in those goals he would like me to pursue for his glory. One of those goals includes this one—a goal to write a book about living life abundantly. Thanks be to God!

Also, I want to express my thanks and love to my family, including my wife, Cathy, for her patience and support, as well as my three children, Anthony, Amanda, and Alexander, for their confidence and trust in me as their father. Without their support and encouragement, this book and this path in our journey of life together may not have been possible. It is to them that this book is dedicated.

I would like to thank everyone that I have had the privilege of knowing in my years in the profession of human resources, including the thousands of employees that I have had the honor to work for. You have inspired me to serve you and search and learn ways that may help all of us to become more successful in our life pursuits.

To those who allowed me my first steps in implementing my dream, including Pastor Sid Gauby, who believed in this mission and provided an opportunity to share it, as well as to Pastor Russ Abel, who kept the dream alive, and to those first attendees to the Live Life Abundantly Workshop, my greatest thanks!

I would like to also thank both my mother and father for providing an environment that allowed me to dream great dreams and to go after anything that I wanted to pursue. Despite my father having died over ten years ago, his drive, ambition, and courage throughout his life have continued to inspire me in my times of trials. Words cannot express my love, appreciation, and admiration for them as parents and for them allowing me to live a life full of goals!

Finally, to those in my life that I have had the honor to know through politics and community and civic organizations, including Bethel United Methodist, Saint Joseph United Methodist, Indiana University—Purdue University at Fort Wayne (IPFW), and the University of Saint Francis to name only a few, you have inspired, encouraged, and provided an opportunity for me to continue to live a life of abundance! Thank you!

INTRODUCTION

It started one night in a quiet hotel room somewhere in North Carolina. I'd been traveling for the company I was working for at that time, keeping up with the grind of the human resources profession. While trying to squeeze a seventy-hour workweek into a forty-hour work schedule, it was becoming obvious to me that the treadmill was going faster, but the destination wasn't changing. It was the same thing year after year. In the quiet of that evening, while praying about life and what God wanted me to do with mine, I had a vision that I believe was inspired by God to create a company based on John 10:10, when Jesus said, "I've come that you may live life more abundantly!" As the vision and idea just kept coming to me and flooded my mind that evening, I pleaded to the Lord, "I have no time to put this idea together! How would I ever try to create this concept when the treadmill of life is going faster by the day, Lord?" It was within weeks of that prayer that my job was surprisingly and abruptly ended! And so it began!

The challenge of goal setting, especially the goals you believe are hand delivered by God, is that you simply cannot give up on them! So while other things—jobs, family, crises, ups and downs of life—kept coming at me, I have continued this pursuit to write this book and launch the Life Planners, Inc. company (LPI) simultaneously. With a severance package in hand, I left my job, and I found that all of a sudden I was provided as much time as I needed to create this company while being paid! God is good!

I guess in a deeper sense it started way before that night because I had been setting goals all my life! Growing up, I had lists of lists of things that I wanted to accomplish for the day, week, month, year, and my entire life. These lists, the techniques to achieve them, and more importantly, my lifetime goals have guided me through a lifetime of blessings and have brought to me a life filled with abundance!

Let me clarify before going further in case we have a different understanding and impression of abundance. Abundance isn't the stuff that we accumulate or hope to have. It isn't the house or the cars, the furniture or collectibles. Rather, abundance is living a life that is fulfilling. A life of abundance is the life that fills that emptiness, sadness, hopelessness that we all experience at times. Abundance is a peace that overcomes you when you know the Lord is watching over you and protecting you. So while we make lists and we have hopes and dreams, the abundance that is referred to in the title and in the pages that follow is that of feeling fulfilled and at peace with God.

The dance, however, between having thousands of goals or simply one goal and then finding peace in the pursuit of achieving it can be difficult. This is because if the goals we set become an obsession, and for many they can, life can easily become overwhelming. The dance, identifying great big goals and yet finding peace, is best accomplished when one has a moral compass to guide them. By the way, maintaining the moral compass is part of the twenty-five-step process of achieving goals. But we'll work out these details in the coming pages. For now, remember that while mentioned hundreds of times in this book, a life of abundance is much, much more than accumulating or achieving stuff!

So with the severance package beginning to run out, I launched the concept and the company. Writing a book, however, would have to wait for several years. But the dream was alive! My thanks to God for helping me realize that you must be careful of what you pray for!

As job opportunities came to me and knowing that the mortgage must be paid, I was blessed to accept a job that allowed me to maintain my life's objectives while I continued my pursuit of this God-driven dream. You know, that's the thing with setting and pursuing goals: you can increase the drive toward achieving one while putting another goal aside until you're ready for it. Now that's exciting! We can choose to challenge ourselves with many goals simultaneously but with different speeds or levels of tenacity! One of the stages of goal achievement is the achievement stage. In this section of the book, you will learn how to set and achieve multiple goals. Though it is toward the end of the book, hang in there because achieving one goal is exciting but several at one time is invigorating!

Having watched ten years go by and my kids growing up, I found myself again challenged through prayer, trying to answer to the Lord when I might write this book. I knew not to ask, through prayer, for more time because of what happened previously, so I didn't. I felt it was time to get started on this God-driven dream, and through prayer, I promised the Lord that I would get moving! The irony was that shortly after this prayer, it happened again! I was surprisingly and abruptly let go from my job! I remembered thinking while being let go, *They* [my bosses] *know not what they do* because the Lord was in control. This time, he even doubled my severance package, allowing me even more time to reach this goal! God is good!

So it was my hope to complete this book so that it might give you some ideas on how you can pursue some God-driven dreams and, above all, to live life abundantly!

Chapter 1

WHY SHOULD I SET GOALS?

One of the most amazing questions that I've come to hear is, "Why should I set goals in my life?" I've been amazed to hear this question both from young and old and from people of all stages of life.

I guess I've been setting goals my entire life. My father, a list maker, was always writing down things he wanted to accomplish. Whether I picked up this behavior from him, I'm not sure. Or was it because I was the third child and I was always trying to impress two older brothers? Or was it because I decided to try to achieve lots of things on my own? Or was it simply that I knew that if you want to either get something in life or achieve something, you need a plan to get there. So, I'm not sure why but it could have been my environment growing up or a biological makeup or possibly both that influenced my "hard-wired" passion to dream and set goals of all sizes and for an entire lifetime.

For me, identifying, setting, and achieving goals is as motivating, exciting, and fulfilling as it might be for an artist to paint, a pilot to fly, a marathoner to run, or an astronaut to leave the planet! Frankly, I'm crazy about setting goals! It isn't even the act of achieving as much as the visioning of what could be.

The funny thing is whether we're aware or not, we all have goals. Some of us may be aware of them; others may not be consciously aware, but they are setting goals probably daily and possibly by the hour. By the time you complete this book, you will be able to focus on specific goals that are either lifetime goals or the smaller ones that need to be accomplished today or by the week's end.

After twenty years of human resources management, I've listened to individuals of all ages and stages of life, coming into my office sharing that they didn't know why they chose a job or career or why they stayed in jobs for ten, twenty, and thirty years. So I began to think about how I can assist individuals to make better annual or even lifetime goals as well as ways to help them achieve them!

So when asked why people should set goals, I respond in a pragmatic sense that it's obvious that while goals help us to get what we want, they also guide us to go to places we want to go. They even allow us to be all that we can be. But in a larger sense, I believe they add flavor, excitement, enthusiasm to life, and they can create and fulfill a zest for life! So while the list for why we should have goals could be endless, I will suggest that there are six reasons everyone should set goals in their lives.

I believe God wants us to set goals in order for us to have a vision for the future!

One of the best reasons to set goals that I can suggest for individuals is I believe God wants us to. There are many examples in the Bible, I believe, that refer to setting goals. While this book on goal setting isn't written to explain or interpret the biblical meanings of the written Word, you can find, I believe, that there are many verses from the Bible that refer to setting goals. In this chapter, I've listed seven verses that I believe point us to setting goals in our lives.

First, in Proverbs 29:18, I believe we see our first example of why goals are important in our lives. It refers to creating visions of where we want to be in life or what we want to achieve. Proverbs 29:18 states, "Where there is no vision the people will cast off restraint." I believe that God wants us to have a vision for our future. This verse simply implies, I believe, that if we don't have a road map, vision, or goal, we may not be able to restrain ourselves in making poor choices. We can easily find people all around us who don't have goals in their lives. Sometimes by not having goals to guide us, we can make bad decisions.

Making bad decisions can lead to bad consequences too. We've heard the expression "The idle mind is the devil's playground." Choosing a path or vision for your life and the decisions you will make toward achieving your goals, if done with God's help, can only lead to a more abundant life!

Another example is Philippians 3:13, which tells us to keep looking forward in life and not to look backward. It states, "But one thing I do, forgetting those things which are behind and reaching forward to those things which are ahead." That is what a goal will do—focus us forward in our lives. Whatever goals we set, whatever our age or stage in life, whatever socioeconomic status we're in, or whatever the size or complexity of the goal, it doesn't matter because goals help us to look forward rather than backward. They help us to forget what is behind us and help us to strain toward what is ahead. I believe that God wants us looking forward in life and enjoying the beauty of accomplishing things while we're on planet Earth for a short time. Looking backward at our trials and tribulations, trips and falls, or even at our failures isn't what I think God wants for us. So today, begin to focus on new goals and a new life ahead and allow God to lead the way!

Philippians 1:6 states, "Being confident of this very thing, that He who has begun a good work in you will complete it." You're not finished! At any age, God continues to help you grow and to live life abundantly! What is it in life do you feel that you haven't yet finished?

As Philippians 3:14 puts it, "I press toward the goal for the prize of the upward call of God in Christ Jesus." By focusing on growing close to God in all that we do, through our goals, we can continue to grow closer to God throughout life.

Proverbs 11:18 reminds us that those who plant what is right will certainly be rewarded! So plant ideas, dreams, and goals that are to do good, and I believe that God will help you achieve them. Those who plant great goals will surely be rewarded, and remember that we reap what we sow! Don't let another day go by without thinking about God-driven dreams and know that we need to continually plant great ideas for our futures!

Matthew 17:20 talks about having faith, "For assuredly, I say to you, if you have faith as a mustard seed, you will say to this mountain, move from here to there, and it will move; and nothing will be impossible for you." Imagine identifying your lifetime goals knowing that God is helping you to select them, and with faith, you can accomplish all of them! It truly makes me think about the importance of what we ask for.

Finally, from John 10:10, Jesus stated, "I've have come that they might have life, and that they might have it more abundantly!" I believe we are to live life to its fullest and, regardless of age or stage in life, to live abundantly! His statement wasn't "I have come that you may live life more abundantly until you're forty-five years of age!" He wants you to live a life of abundance for your entire life.

Everything we have in life was a goal!

Think about it, everything you see in existence that has been made by man was a goal that someone had. This book, the chair you're in, the room, the house, your neighborhood, the town and the state that you're living in, or even the nation that you're in was a goal! From the pyramids, bridges, highways, castles, and the seven wonders of the world, everything was a goal for those who achieved it! For these accomplishments to have happened, they had to be someone's vision and goal to complete. I get so excited thinking that while we didn't know the leaders, rulers, or kings throughout the history of the world, we have something very much in common with all of them—we can dream and visualize and set goals just as they did! Without goals, life is a treadmill (which in a literal sense also was a goal for someone!) and will simply become a routine. In a routine life we lack the challenge and potential that, as humans we have. Goals provide us the potential and ability to identify, set and achieve greatness!

Goals help us in the tough times of life by providing us hope!

Another reason that I believe everyone should have goals in life is that goals can help us to persevere during the tough times in life. Life is full of problems, challenges, calamities, disasters, and catastrophes that seem to come at unexpected times or stages in our lives. Whether you're facing one of those times now or in the future, goals can help to get you through those times. By knowing that your life, your existence, and your overall influence or purpose in life are bigger than any problem you're facing, you can plan to achieve life's goals far beyond any current-day crisis you may be experiencing.

You see, I believe that goals provide a sense of hope. Hope, I also believe, is a God-given mental state, and by having hope and faith, we can get through any problem we are currently faced with. If you look at societies today, many people have lost the overall sense of hope. I'm not suggesting that they are in a sense of despair overall; rather, that some simply are lacking goals in their lives and, as a result, not experiencing hope either. As a result, without consciously knowing it, they play the lottery in order to experience that sense of excitement and the hope that comes with holding that ticket with them weekly. In fact, at the time this book was written, the Mega Millions Lottery was setting another record, and people throughout the United States were buying tickets everywhere and at a record pace. That feeling, that buzz, that euphoria of something that could happen in the future and that they have a chance of that something is actually a sense of hope. I believe and I know from those who have set goals that goals can and will do the same thing for you, and you have a much better chance of achieving your goals than winning the lottery!

Another example of enjoying the sense of hope may be with the various sports teams in every community across the country. By supporting football, basketball, baseball and hockey teams at the collegiate level or pro level, we gain a sense of hope and, thereby, excitement in our lives. Goals can do the same thing and may not cost you as much cash as those season tickets or lost opportunities! Meaning, rather than you waiting for something to occur without you having any influence on its outcome, goals allow you to drive, guide, and influence their outcomes and successes. This then gives you a sense of hope and accomplishment! They can provide a sense of guidance in difficult times and will give you unconsciously a sense of hope for the future. Your mind will automatically begin to focus on how you will achieve the goals that you've set for yourself. So while fighting physical and/or mental injuries and illnesses, relationship difficulties, financial setbacks or even financial ruin, academic failures, job loss, or even feelings of spiritual emptiness, by setting goals for a future state rather than a current state, we create a sense of hope in our lives. That sense of hope coupled with faith will provide a way through our problems and ultimately help us achieve all that we want to achieve.

So if you think you don't have goals because you're not feeling positive or optimistic about your chances of achieving them, by setting goals, you gain a sense of hope and, thereby, enhance your outlook in life, which results in increasing your belief of your chances in reaching your goals!

Goals help us achieve things!

The practical view of goal setting is that if you want something, you simply need to plan for it. If we want to get something in life, we simply need to visualize it and then plan to achieve it! From setting goals such as; to complete a journey, or learning goals, or educational goals, or career goals, or spiritual goals, we simply need to identify the plan, and we can make things happen. The challenge in goal setting though, is to identify what roadblocks that you'll have to get over, go around or plow through to achieve your goal! Ultimately, goals can help us achieve the things in life we want to achieve or acquire things we want to obtain.

Goals can help us find out what we're good at!

Socrates said, "The unexamined life is not worth living." His philosophy is, why not try everything! Wow, think of it, to live a life full of exploration and adventure! Goals will help us to live a life of challenges and excitement resulting in learning what we're good at. Learning what we're good at can in turn sustain a zest for living life! By creating a goal that requires us to do something we've never done before, we can learn through trial and error what we're good at. I truly believe that we are capable of achieving anything we want as long as we're doing it for the right reason. It seems a bit simplistic, probably is, but I believe life is about setting goals. Without a vision, a plan, a goal, we simply exist, and I believe this can be a dangerous and huge waste of our God-given potential. So, set a goal and you can find out what you're good at.

Goals help us figure out what we're passionate about in life!

Trying to understand our passions in life can actually be figured out by identifying and setting goals. Some may suggest that we only need to set goals in areas of our passions. However, I would suggest by identifying the places we want to go, the career we want in life, the kind of mother or father we want to be, we can actually help ourselves to better understand what areas of life we are most passionate about. Later, we'll explore the balanced goal-setting process by setting various goals in several categories in your life. By doing so, you'll begin to identify areas that you are most excited about. These areas of passion, just like your goals, can and will change in life, but you'll be able to figure them out by establishing goals in all aspects of life.

So if you're asking why you should set goals, I believe there are more reasons to set goals than I could possibly print in this book. But in order to make the case, let me just review the few that we've covered.

I believe that God wants you to create a vision for your future! Another reason to set goals is to recognize that life, and nearly everything in it, has been a goal for someone. By setting your goals, you can overcome the challenges in life that come your way, whatever they are presently or whatever may come at you later in life. Also, I know that there are things you want to accomplish, and goals will help you to achieve them. If you don't know what you're best at in life, goals can help you figure that out too! Goals will also bring a sense of hope back into your life. Goals will take a lackluster life and make it a roaring adventure! Ultimately, goals will enhance your life, enlarge your life, and help you achieve what you want to obtain, and through it all, they will help you to live life abundantly!

Chapter 1
Why Set Goals?

- ✓ *I believe God wants us to set goals to have a vision for our future!*
  The Bible is full of references I believe that show us that we are to create goals throughout our entire life. Which verse is the most meaningful to you?

- ✓ *Everything we have in life was a goal!*
  The book you're reading, the chair you're in or e-reader you're using, the city or town, state or nation . . . were all goals at one time. Everything achieved was a goal for someone . . . so goals are the essence of life! Pick any item, product, company, or world event and research it to learn whose goal it was.

- ✓ *Goals help us in the tough times of life by providing us hope!*
  Right now, you may be experiencing some tough challenges in your life. These challenges could be dealing with health issues, relationships, financial difficulties or you simply wonder why life can be so difficult. Goals create hope in our life so whatever you're challenged with . . . set a goal to overcome your adversity and you'll find hope returning to your life. What difficulty are you experiencing that you could set a goal to conquer?

- ✓ *Goals help us achieve things!*
  New clothes, shoes, bike, car, house, a date, a friend, a customer, a vacation . . . whatever we want to achieve in life, goals can take and deliver us there! What is it that you want to achieve right now?

- ✓ *Goals help us find out what we're good at!*
  What aspect of life are you good at? Is it your spiritual life, physical and mental state, educational accomplishments, family and social successes, career achievements, financial status, or being adventurous? If you're not sure what areas you're good or best at try to set goals in all of these areas to determine what you're good at.

✓ *Goals help us figure out what we're passionate about!*
Sometimes life can become routine and goals can help us identify what we're most passionate about. If you know what you're passionate about set goals in those areas. If you don't know what your passion is, by setting goals in various aspects of your life, you can identify your new passions!

Chapter 2

WHAT GOALS SHOULD I SET?

So many choices and so little time—that is the challenge for goal setters! Identifying what goals to set can be a challenge in itself. If you're saying at this point "I have no clue what goals I'm interested in" or "I haven't had a chance to set many goals," just hang in there. We'll go through some specific goals in this chapter that will help you.

Whatever you do, don't fall into a "goallessness" state! Those who don't set goals can find themselves with few challenges resulting in little achievement. With limited risks and challenges in life, one may not be able to live a life of abundance. Those that choose not to have goals, or do not identify, set or pursue goals can find themselves feeling empty, lost and passionless. I refer to this as a "goal deficit disorder" (GDD). We've heard the expression "If you don't know where you're at, it's hard to know where you're going." I would flip this around to say, "If you don't know where you're going, it's hard to know where you're at."

So to identify a path for your future and thereby help to figure out where you're at presently, choose a different path by selecting a God-driven-dream! (GDD) That's right, the same letters but an entirely different outcome. Now the question to ask as we begin to think about goals is, "what goals should I set?"

Sometimes, those that help to teach goal setting will suggest that with a piece of paper and thirty seconds, you can write down those things that come to mind, and these become your primary goals. These topics, ideas, and dreams that you identify by writing down, are the only ones you should focus on. While I don't disagree in using this approach, I believe it leaves one only to focus on those things that are in the forefront of one's thoughts. Further, it doesn't balance your goals for a lifetime of achievement. In this chapter, we'll go through a more thorough approach by identifying fourteen areas in your life to set goals.

Set goals that help you with today's problems!

One of the areas that goals can be set is with the immediate challenges facing us in our lives. These goals could come from the thirty-second exercise mentioned previously. Or they could include any given crisis or problem, including illnesses, a sense of overall emptiness, being in between jobs or careers, financial difficulties, marriage and family difficulties, deciding whether to purchase a new car because the current one is failing, fighting health concerns, trying to decide what school to send your children to, or trying to pass a required course. These are just a few examples of problems you may be facing. So if you're experiencing difficulties in any area of your life, you may set goals to find a resolution or a path through whatever you're challenged with. Goals can help you through the anxiety, stress, and helplessness that you may be experiencing.

Set goals that influence your passions!

Another way goals can be created could come from one's passions in life. If we find that family is our priority in life, we'll find that we can easily identify goals in this area. How to best raise our children, how to provide for their education, what schools they should attend, what courses they should choose, how the family should spend their vacation together, or even how to teach our children the process of setting goals are some simple examples for focusing on family goals. If you're an adventurist, you might choose goals that include what new sport you want to play, where to go on vacation, what new topic or game to learn, or what new experiences you would like to achieve in your life. If your career is your passion, you may be focused on gaining a new client, starting your own business, improving your leadership skills, receiving a raise or promotion, or achieving a new professional certification or designation.

Ultimately, you can use your passions in life to help you identify goals that you should set in your life.

Set goals based on your age and stage in life!

Your age or stage in life can be another way to determine what kind of goals you could consider. If you're in your younger years (high school years), you know that there are fundamental goals that need to be achieved that include attending school, passing your classes, and ultimately, completing a high school education. Finding that first job or first bike or first car, having the first date, being selected to the club or sports team, opening your first savings account, deciding whether you should go to college, deciding what college you should attend—it seems the number of objectives and goals to set are endless at this stage! If you're completing college or recently married, again, there are lots of goals to be made. These goals can include the following questions: What job should I apply for? What company should I work for? Where should I live? Should I rent a house or apartment or buy a house? What should I do for transportation? Should we marry in the spring or summer? Should it be an indoor or outdoor wedding? Again, the list of goals to set seems to be endless.

Later as life becomes very busy, however, you may begin to ask, "How can I accomplish anything if I am simply trying to keep up with the day-to-day to-do list?" Setting goals at this stage that help to balance the numerous demands in your life can be productive and even therapeutic. Or having raised the family and now finding the home becoming quiet and the clock slowing, allowing you to do things you thought you'd never be able to get to do, you may now feel that you have the opportunity to set some significant life-achieving goals. These goals might include growing closer to God, traveling, relaxing, completing your educational pursuits, or losing those twenty pounds you've been trying to lose for several years.

You may be at a stage in your life in which you want to set goals for your retirement. Goals including financial income, health, and fitness, traveling or where to live, deciding what kind of a grandparent you want to be, or how can you give something back to your community come to mind. Retirement, as it's been thought of, is now being redefined by the baby boomers that are entering into this stage with new ideas, expectations, and goals! Use the stage of life you're in or about to be in to determine meaningful goals in life!

So whether it's the crisis, the passion, or the stage in life that helps us to determine goals, one of the keys to success, as I've learned, is balancing the kinds of goals we're pursuing. Balance in life and in one's goals and pursuits has been said to be the recipe for success in life. Whatever age or stage we're at, we ultimately need to keep a balance in the types of goals we set and attempt to achieve. By spending all our time and effort toward a single goal in life, we're bound to damage or sacrifice some other aspect and importance in life. We're all too familiar with the example of the businessman who spent his life being successful at the business resulting in missing the children growing up, the marriage beginning to fail and even missing the raising of his grandchildren only to realize while on his deathbed, that he blew it by not spending more time with his family! So if balance is the answer to being successful, what goals should be set? And what does "balance" in goal setting mean?

When we think about life and try to identify goals in various aspects of it, we will many times find words that fall into the following categories: spiritual, physical, mental, educational, family, social, career, financial, and adventure. These categories have been identified by writers, authors, and philosophers in many different ways. For the purpose of this book and for discussion, feel free to modify these titles as you wish, but generally, these areas are commonly understood with the titles listed. The adventure category is one that I have broken into further groupings because it can mean so much for so many of us. Under the category of adventure, we will use the following four areas: exploration, sports/art, learning, and experiencing. Each of these, as well as the major categories, will be described in the following pages.

You can better balance your life by identifying goals in the following areas:

Spiritual Goals

One of the first areas for consideration of setting goals is the category of spiritual goals. Choosing the spiritual category first isn't by random choice. In fact, choosing to set goals with God first seems to make the entire process exactly right. Spiritual goals can establish a foundation of one's life that makes everything else fall together perfectly. This doesn't mean, however, that you'll have a perfect life without challenges; rather, by establishing spiritual goals, you can create a life where God gives you some remarkable goals to achieve. Then he will guide you (if you let him) along the way to achieve them! Examples of goals in this area can range from deepening your relationship with your creator to working on a mission's project, reading the entire Bible or praying daily. These goals can add to the richness in life that can, above all else, fill the emptiness that we experience at times in life.

One of the goals that I set early in my life was to be active in whatever church I belonged to. It would also be important to have my entire family also growing closer to the church. I set a goal to learn more about my religion and establish a foundation of faith in my family. To do this, I felt that I needed to find a church that the family liked and that was convenient to attend and then create some involvement for each family member. Goals that I set included becoming a lay speaker for the United Methodist Church as well as being active with the church. This goal has led me to being on church boards, leading youth groups, coordinating mission projects, and more recently, playing drums in praise bands for my church. By achieving these goals, I achieved much, much more than I anticipated because throughout the pursuit, all three of my children stayed active in the church's youth group and have developed a faith-filled life too.

Physical and Mental Health Goals

Setting goals for physical and mental wellness is next. It seems as if these types of goals are made annually by most and also forgotten by most by the middle of February! When you're considering physical and mental goals, remember that speaking to your doctor prior to any exercise program would be advisable and recommended. We may think that we're in great shape now, but the risk is that while initially the goal for diet and exercise isn't too hard, as we increase the intensity of working out or dieting, we can begin to challenge parts of our body that aren't ready for this. Mental wellness goals can include finding peace, joy, and calmness that allow you to relax or even improve your self-esteem.

Before I could begin writing this book, I made a goal to lose over twenty-five pounds and felt I couldn't write this book until I accomplished it. How could I possibly write a book on achieving goals, if I couldn't set and achieve a goal to lose twenty-five pounds? After six months of intensive, old-fashion work outs, running, and elliptical workouts, I reached my goal. I am now able to write a book on achieving goals and feel confident about it! Ultimately, achieving both mental and physical goals that keep you in good condition will also help you to accomplish many other lifetime goals that require you to be healthy and fit.

Educational Goals

Educational goals can be set at any age or stage in our lives. Whether it's completing ninth grade English to completing a PhD or anything in between, we can create a life of learning by establishing goals in the area of education. Educational goals have been some of the most rewarding for me throughout life. These goals have allowed me an opportunity to learn, which is a passion of mine. Educational goals are goals that fit in to more formalized academic instruction. Informal learning or individualized learning will fit into the adventure goals and under the learning category that we'll cover a bit later. Think of classes, courses, diplomas, certifications and degrees for this category. These kinds of educational pursuits can be tied to your career and vocation goals, or they can simply be areas that you would like to pursue. Selecting educational goals can be exciting and can add value to your life at all ages!

Family and Social Goals

Whether young or old, we have all come from families. We may have created our own family, or may be contemplating settings goals for a family we plan to create in the future. These goals can include everything from growing closer together to family members, creating a family game night or movie night, learning a new hobby together, spending more time with grandparents or grandchildren or even to set goals of when you have a family in the future, or planning what to do to create some fond memories together. Setting goals to mend damaged relationships or to simply make sure you don't miss your mother or father's birthday each year can make for a meaningful goal to achieve as well. You can begin today to visualize your family of the future or to mend some current hurts, or to build a stronger family relationship.

Despite whatever age or stage you are at or whatever your relationship is as a family member presently, we all have needs to create and maintain friendships beyond family as well. These relationships can fall into social goals. Social goals include making a new friend, joining local professional clubs, attending neighborhood groups, participating in networking organizations, going out on a date once a week or month, or meeting with friends monthly. These can be worthy objectives for social goals. How often do we think to make new friends or expand the number of people we associate with on a regular basis? By creating a goal to be a better friend or make a new friend each month, you can add value to your social goals and provide a meaningful life for you and those new acquaintances you meet as well!

Financial Goals

When it comes to money, it seems all of us have dreams, wishes, and goals, though we need to make more goals and make fewer wishes! Setting financial goals is exciting because there are so many goals that can be set. First, we can set goals for the amount we want to earn based on the lifestyle we are planning to live or even where we want to live. We can set goals to determine how we're going to earn income. Goals can be set to increase investment, how much we want to put into our 401(k) account, and how much our weekly expenses should be as a ratio to our income. These kinds of goals can be set to reduce debt, increase savings, and even to decrease the number of credit cards we have. Financial goals can include what we want to have available for retirement to even what we expect to leave our beneficiaries.

I remember setting at the age of twenty-four how much I planned to make in five—and ten-year increments for the next thirty years. I knew that I had to make a certain amount to live the style of life I wanted to live. Thanks be to God because I was able to achieve and exceed this goal almost the entire thirty years! I remember at a very young age setting a goal to give $25 a week to my church. As my income grew, I prayed to the Lord that I would continue to give more, and I have grown this amount extensively with God's help! There are more than enough goals we can identify in the area of finance, but realize that with balance, they can be appropriately focused on.

Career Goals

One of the areas that I have learned where we can set better goals is in the area of our careers. After twenty years in human resources, I have consulted many times with individuals who were not sure of why they chose the career path that they were in or why they stayed in the job for as long as they did. Most of the time, they started a career or took a job not by choice but by necessity. This has been obviously successful for many, but if you're asking questions about your career or the field that you have either chosen or landed in by default, you may need to identify more meaningful goals in this area.

So as you explore career goals, they can range from the first paper-route job as a twelve-year-old to determining what vocation you'll choose for the rest of your life. A goal in this area can include choosing a mind-set such as are you living to work or are you working to live? Ultimately, career goals can bring wonderful opportunities to contribute in your profession and provide a source of income that can allow you to achieve other goals too.

Within this context, you can begin to break down these goals into smaller goals in which you're picking where to work, which industry to work in, where the job will be located, how long you want to stay with a company or job or even an industry. Details about reaching milestones within your career, including certifications, degrees, and awards, can be goals that can be set as well.

Having goals for your profession or job can help you navigate through the ups and downs of your career. It can help you during job transitions, job promotions, being offered new opportunities in your career and whether to veer off one career path to accept another. Career goals can also include work as a volunteer for agencies and organizations. By establishing goals to lead a PTA group, become the president of your neighborhood board of directors, build a house for Habitat for Humanity, or even be the treasurer for your son's Boy Scout troop, you can help to build your résumé and help to use your vocation to help others. There will be lots of roadblocks, turns, curves, and occasional cliffs to navigate through in your career but goals will help you to reach your identified career path objectives.

Adventure Goals

If you do not have any adventure goals identified presently, regardless of your age or stage, now is the time that you need to set adventure goals! These goals make life fun and will even help to make life more exciting too! They can include any goal not finding its home in the previous categories. However, I have broken these into the following groupings: exploration, sports/art, learning, and experiencing.

Exploration

These goals include places you would like to see, visit, or even to live. I set a goal early in my life to visit all the fifty states of the United States before I was fifty years-old. I remember writing this goal thinking how in the world would I ever make it to Hawaii or Alaska! But before the age of fifty, my children's marching band had been invited to Hawaii to perform! And as part of our twenty-fifth wedding anniversary, my wife and I decided to take a cruise to Alaska. (Taking a cruise to Alaska was a goal too!) By the way, as part of the family goals, we even decided to take all three of our children with us!

My wife and I decided early that we enjoyed traveling and decided to purchase a membership into a travel club. The idea is that you pay a lot of money up front, and then over time, you can travel places relatively inexpensively throughout the United States and even worldwide. We did this even before we had decided on the places we wanted to travel to. We built into our life plan the opportunity to continue to travel. Before we knew it, we were planning family vacations to the West and Northeast, allowing us to travel as a family and reaching parts of the country we never thought we would be able to explore.

Keep challenging yourself to go places or see things throughout your life that you've not seen before. It makes life fun, and you will continue to learn how small our world really is.

Sports/Art

This category of sports and art came together for those that want to either participate in or learn various sports and/or would prefer to participate in creating and/or learning about art. If you want to study famous painters, sculptors, and musicians or visit art museums, these goals can easily fit into this grouping. For those choosing sports, they may choose to learn how to play rugby or figure out how to win at chess. There are more than enough sport and art topics to participate in and learn for a lifetime, so why not plan some goals for a balance in both. I decided to take up biking one year and bought my wife and me our own bikes. Initially, they didn't get much use, but a few years later, I was able to complete a fifty-mile bike ride with my youngest son! He was completing a merit badge for Boy Scouts, and the trip, the biking, and the event was priceless and will never be forgotten! Take up a sport for yourself with a significant other, with a friend, with your wife or children, and you'll never know when the knowledge of that sport will come in handy or help you to help someone else complete their goals too!

Learning

As a human resources professional, I've come to a conclusion that lifetime learning is essential for continued success and good mental and physical health too. So why not plan to continue to learn for a lifetime! You could identify goals in this category literally for the rest of your life! Anything that comes to mind, including hobbies, specific interests, cultures, and academic subjects, can fit into the learning category. From learning the various currencies of the world, learning different languages, learning the history of the Greek civilization, or learning to raise exotic fish, there is no limit to what we can continue to learn while on planet Earth! Each year, pick a new topic and continue to learn throughout your lifetime! A fun goal in this category is learning how to cook several cuisines. Mexican food, Italian food, Chinese food, and German food are a few that come to mind. The completion of this book that you're now reading has come with lots of learning about how to write and publish a book, a goal that I set over twenty years ago! Whatever you choose, keep learning, and life will reward you for doing so.

Experiencing

This group of goals can be some of the most meaningful of the goals in life. These types of goals can include experiencing a feeling, a moment, an emotion, or watching something occur or take place. What do you want to experience in life? I set a goal to watch the sun rise over Rocky Mountain National Park at fourteen thousand feet! Later, I expanded this goal to watching the sunrise at all four corners of our country, so from West Palm Beach, Maine, Southern California, and Seattle, I've made it a point to see and experience the sunrise in each of these locations. Another goal that I set was to go to the Vietnam Memorial and be there alone as the sun came up. It was an experience I will never forget! There have been many fun ones too that included riding every roller coaster at Cedar Point and having my foot land on the bricks on the Indianapolis 500 raceway while running a minimarathon!

Joy, peace, comfort, compassion, and contentment are wonderful emotions to achieve in life! Setting goals that include giving to others, slowing the schedule for the family commitments, or simply focusing on others can lead to a more positive emotional life for all involved. Think of how you can help others experience these feelings and emotions too.

So when asking yourself, "What goals should I set?" remember there are more than enough to add excitement and abundance to your life! We'll have a chance to identify some of them in the coming chapters. Hopefully, by now you've started to think of some goals that you've always wanted to pursue. If so, write them down. Don't put it off. Write them on the dream sheet pages in the appendix of this book or even in the margins, but get them written down, and we'll begin to explore ways you *will* achieve them in the coming chapters!

Life Planners Inc. provides a Life Achievement Planner to write all your lifetime goals in, and it can be purchased at *www.lifeplannersnow.com*. Along with the value of writing these goals down, you will also be able to share them with your children and grandchildren through your own personal Life Achievement Planner. A memory and a lifetime of amazing goals are worth sharing!

Now that we've discussed the kinds of goals to achieve, the remainder of this book will focus on how to identify dreams, how to turn them into goals, and finally, how to achieve them!

Chapter 2
What Kind of Goals Should I Set?

✓ *Not knowing what goals to set could lead to GDD!*
By not setting goals at all, or not having a balance of goals in your life, you could experience what I call a "goal-deficit-disorder!" So to overcome the emptiness of a GDD, try setting some God-driven-dreams instead!

✓ *Set goals that help you with today's problems.*
We've all got them... so why not set goals to help yourself with the problems that you're challenged with today? Think about any of the challenges that exist in your life today, right now, and set goals to triumph over them.

✓ *Set goals that influence your passions.*
What aspect of life are you most passionate and enthusiastic about? If you could choose to do anything you wanted right now... what would it be? Once you can answer that question, why not set goals around this area?

✓ *Set goals based on your age and stage in life.*
Whatever age or stage you are in your life there are goals that need to be set. Think about your age (and what age you feel like) and set goals based on your age or stage. If you're younger and starting a family what goals can you set? If you're nearing retirement set goals based on what you would like to do with the extra time in your life.

Balance your lifetime with goals in the following areas:

✓ *Spiritual Goals*
What goals have you set for improving your spiritual life?

✓ *Physical and Mental Health Goals*
What goals have you set for a lifetime of mental and physical health?

- ✓ *Educational Goals*
  What goals have you set to achieve educational pursuits in your life? From degrees, certificates, licenses and even courses on various subjects, a lifetime of educational goals keeps you growing mentally and professionally.

- ✓ *Family and Social Goals*
  What goals have you set for your family or your social life? To help your family members or friends achieve their goals can be very rewarding!

- ✓ *Financial Goals*
  What are the financial goals you want to set? How much debt or income do you want?

- ✓ *Career Goals*
  What career or job goals have you set? What one goal comes to mind when you think about your job?

- ✓ *Adventure Goals*
  - Exploration: Set goals to explore places, locations, cities, states and countries!
  - Sports/Art: Set goals to participate in and learn several sports and various fields of art.
  - Learning: Set goals to keep learning about all kinds of topics for a lifetime!
  - Experiencing: Set goals to experience a feeling, a moment, an emotion or to watch something occur or take place.

Chapter 3

THE GOAL-SETTING PROCESS

One of the most exciting aspects of life is the process of identifying, setting, and achieving goals! This process doesn't just happen however. Some might consider that simply wishing for a dream to come to true is how the process works. I believe wishing is about dreaming, but once a dream is written down, it becomes a goal!

Diagram 3.1. The LPI goal-setting diagram

The LPI goal-setting diagram

The art of achieving goals isn't about wishing, and it isn't about luck either! I also believe that those who achieve goals don't just think of them to remain in their minds. I believe and studies have shown that for successful goal achievers to reach their goals, first, they think of them, but then they also write them down! By moving ideas from our minds to a written form, we're making the conscious step to say we're going to achieve this either sooner or later! By writing our goals down, we're able to coordinate our efforts toward achieving them along with the other thousands of demands in our lives. When asked, "How did you achieve this goal?" those who achieved goals might respond, "Well, I just kept thinking about it." While this may be true, I believe that it goes further than that. I believe there is a process or system of identifying, setting, and achieving goals. Without this overall process, we'll have ideas and goals that enter our mind but then exit, never to be attempted! By writing down those dreams and ideas, turning them into goals, and then establishing a process to evaluate them throughout your life, you'll be able to pursue the meaningful goals and correctly prioritize the less meaningful ones. This will move you from dreaming, wishing, hoping, or guessing whether you might achieve your goals to identifying ways you will accomplish them!

The process of goal setting includes dreaming, turning your dreams into goals, identifying whether these are short-term or lifetime goals, and creating steps and plans to achieve them. The process is continual in that while you're dreaming about one goal in life, you may be planning to execute how to obtain another goal while you're achieving even a different goal all simultaneously. So as you see from the diagram 3.1, the LPI system of setting goals doesn't stop at any point; rather, it is continual.

So let's start at the beginning when those ideas and dreams just pop into our minds! One of the questions that I am asked is, "When a thought enters my mind, should I consider this a new goal?" This question gets to the heart of why we need a goal-setting process! Whether we're driving or stuck in traffic, in the grocery store or a daughter's soccer game, at work, daydreaming in class, or inspired in church from the pastor's sermon, we're constantly getting thoughts and ideas on what we may want to set as a goal or choose to pursue in the future. So when these thoughts and ideas come to us, are these our new goals? These thoughts and ideas could become goals but should be put through a process to determine if they're "goal-worthy." We'll discuss the evaluation portion of goal setting in the following pages. For now, the process requires writing all these ideas and goals down so you can better evaluate them later.

One exception might be for younger children. When they say they want to be a farmer, fireman, police officer, or schoolteacher, I would consider these as goals. Help them to write it down and hold on to their dream and goal until the next one comes up. By teaching them to move their ideas from thinking it to writing it, you will help them for a lifetime!

Even before we write these ideas down, we begin the process of dreaming great dreams! The first step then is to create an environment to dream! The environment that is needed is not just focused on location; it is also a state of mind. An environment to dream is where you find your mind is clear of stress so that you can think big about your future! This isn't necessarily found while sitting in traffic or being in a stressed state of mind. You will need to explore what environment would be best for you to dream great dreams. You could find that sitting in a boat on calm waters, sitting on a hillside, having beautiful music to listen to, or having nothing but birds and nature sounds can provide you with a sense of serenity that creates your environment to dream great dreams! Sitting in your favorite chair in your front room or sitting on your porch or visiting a local park on a Sunday afternoon could be best for you to set the environment to dream too. Find a place where you can go, be at peace, and clear your mind of current-day thinking. Begin to think about what you've always wanted to do and be, the places you've always wanted to go to, and the person you wanted to be when you grew up. Be careful not to let negative thoughts enter in! Don't try to justify why you haven't completed something in the past or why you couldn't fix problems years ago or your past faults. Rather, remain positive and only think about the things you've wanted to achieve in your life, and then focus on your future. As these ideas come, write them down immediately. Don't try to evaluate them or don't worry that someone is going to see them or even that you might be personally judged based on your list of dreams. This list is for you and isn't meant to be shown or discussed with others. It is for you!

Dream Great Dreams by Letting God In!

One of surest ways you can dream great dreams is to make sure that your dreams and ultimately your goals are big enough to need God to achieve them! When thinking about your dreams, include a prayer that invites God in and ask for guidance, direction, and ideas that will draw you closer to him. Think about what God wants you to do and how you can glorify his name, and the ideas, dreams, and goals will begin to come to you! I believe God wants you to live a life of abundance and is ready to help you dream great dreams to get you there! But most of the time, when we think about setting goals in our lives, we don't bring God into the process. We may think, "I surely don't want to fail, and if God wants me to accomplish this and I fail, yikes!" But flip this thinking around and ask, "Lord, I believe you want me to accomplish this goal, and having you with me, who could possibly be against me?" If you're praying with God and have faith, God will give you ideas and ways to accomplish your goal! Remember, though, God's timeline isn't always our timeline. So sometimes you'll need to be patient and wait before you accomplish a goal, or maybe you're saying you'll work on this goal in five years when God is telling you now is the time to achieve it! Let God in through prayer, and you will dream great dreams!

Dream Your Dreams by Category.

Sometimes it is difficult to just wait for dreams and ideas to come into your mind. So one way to get mentally focused on your lifetime goals and dreams is to think about them by categories that were mentioned in the previous chapter. By thinking of your lifetime goals in terms of spiritual life, your physical and mental health, education, family and social life, career, your finances as well as the adventures of your life, you can allow for some great things to enter! By using the *dream sheets* located in the appendix, you can write down any dreams that come to mind as you're reading this book. Take time now to find these dream sheets in the appendix if you wish to begin by writing dreams for each of the categories listed. You can also return later as you're reading the book and continue to write new dreams down that come to mind even after you finish reading this book.

One final thought about dreaming great dreams is that in the confines of our own mind, we can dream great dreams, and nobody has to know what we're committed to. We can take on the boss, rule the town, own the mansion, become the philanthropist, launch our business, charter a boat down the Amazon, or even live longer than the doctor told us we were going to without anyone knowing what we're dreaming! I believe dreaming is a God-given ability! It's how all the great accomplishments of mankind have occurred! However, it's interesting to me that many times in society the dreamer gets a bad rap! Instead of society being positive and optimistic, many times it's the opposite, and we find cynicism and pessimism controlling our emotions and those around us! Meaning, as soon as an idea enters, a negative thought follows it, "Surely you're not going to try this" or "You're dreaming!" The challenge at this stage of dreaming great dreams is not to think through your dreams but rather to just get them written down! There will be plenty of time for those negative emotions or cynics to be dealt with once you begin to achieve your goal. We'll discuss that later in the book.

Evaluate Your Dreams.

Now that you have thought about your dreams and written them down (I'm trusting that you did take time to write them down), you will now begin to evaluate your dreams. By moving them from dreams on your dream sheets to a timeline to accomplish, they become goals. Some of these goals will be lifetime goals, and others simply will become annual or even monthly goals. The challenge is to determine if the goals should be a lifetime goal or one that you should attempt now and can achieve in weeks or months. Think about the category of the dreams, your skills, and background, and then determine whether these dreams can be accomplished in a lifetime, a few years, or even consider if you can achieve the goal this year.

Make sure that as you are evaluating your dreams you also move your goals from the dream sheets to the Life Achievement Chart and the Annual Achievement Charts in the Appendix. Before going forward, we need to differentiate between a to-do list and goals that would be considered in the context of this book. Those things that we need to do—renewing the driver's license, dropping off the car for repairs, fixing the screen on the back door, or even picking up milk before coming home—while these could be considered goals, this book and the goals referred to in it are actually meant to be more meaningful and are much more than the daily or weekly to-do task list that we're always having to complete. An important exception, however, could be that by setting larger, more meaningful goals for your home, finances, family, to list just a few, you would need to complete several smaller, less significant goals to accomplish the bigger ones, so you may need to establish these as subgoals.

Lifetime Goals

Lifetime dreams or goals sometimes are referred to as items on the bucket list (referring to things you want to accomplish before you kick the bucket); however, I would rather refer to these as those goals that are big and meaningful that you want to do to live life to its fullest! These goals should be those that require extensive time, financing, education, or physical demands. Goals in this area could include lifetime decisions, such as career choices, higher education pursuits, owning your home, traveling to Australia, family planning, or even losing one hundred pounds. Any goal that exceeds five years should become a lifetime goal. By putting it into this category (lifetime goals), you recognize that these types of goals will take a little or a lot longer to achieve. Further, these goals sometimes require you to achieve other things prior to tackling these goals. Many times we see annual goals or sometimes five-year goals change, but the lifetime goals won't change as much. Although, they may require you to put them off for a year or several years before you have the resources to pursue them.

Two-Year to Four-Year Goals

Some goals won't take a lifetime but cannot be accomplished or even started this year for various reasons. Possibly, you need to make changes in your life now to allow you to pursue these goals, or you have to reach initial goals before you can pursue the larger goals. It could be that you want to improve your health by losing weight before you begin an active exercise program, or you need to complete school before you can focus on your career goals, or you want to reduce your debt before you begin to travel the world! Whatever the reason, sometimes goals can fit into the two-year to four-year goal timelines because they cannot be done this year, but you intend to begin and complete them inside of four years. Remember, you cannot accomplish everything in a year, so pace yourself and consider those goals that will take a few years to reach and then place them into this time frame.

Annual Goals

Any goals that can be reached inside a year can be listed in the annual goals time frame. Even if a goal can be accomplished in thirty days, list it as an annual goal. Losing twenty pounds, getting the annual raise on your job, getting a new job, paying off a credit card, taking more walks with your husband or wife or children, or even joining the neighborhood association are examples of those that could easily fit into the annual goal category. Regardless of the time of year you're beginning this process, follow the calendar year as it will keep your goals in an orderly and easy-to-follow format. So if you're beginning this in June or November, it can still be an annual goal.

Monthly Goals

Once you've determined your annual goals, you'll then need to identify from the annual goals list those goals that you'll be able to achieve in the next thirty days or remainder of the month that you're in. Many times these monthly goals are the beginning of many of your annual goals, two—to four-year goals, or lifetime goals. While you may not be able to complete reading the Bible in thirty days, you can first begin to read it! You may not be able to travel to all fifty states in the next year or even the next four years, but you can visit the state adjacent to the one you live in in the next thirty days. So when you begin to list your monthly goals, remember, you don't have to complete something in all categories, but you can take those initial steps in the next thirty days or the remainder of the month you're in.

Weekly Goals

Now the weekly goals are the ones that challenge you to make things happen. You may not be able to complete a college degree in four years or begin to take classes this year, you may not even be ready to register for classes this month, but you could call the admissions office and schedule an appointment to discuss your educational interests. And you can make that call or set that appointment this week! You may not be able to play golf on Hilton Head Island this year, but you can Google the golf courses on the island this week to find out the cost and availability of normal tee-times in the spring of next year. Whatever the goal, you can establish initial steps, including each of the steps in the planning stage (covered in the next chapter) of goal setting beginning as early as *this week!*

The Twenty-Five LPI Goal-Achieving Techniques.

Now that you've identified some goals, evaluated them to determine the timelines you'll begin to pursue them and the estimates of when you will achieve them, we'll now begin to focus on the twenty-five goal-achieving techniques in the remaining chapters of the book. The twenty-five steps will be identified and explained within the four stages (planning and mental, action, persistence, and achievement) of goal achievement.

Dream More Dreams.

As mentioned previously, the art of dreaming and subsequently establishing meaningful goals in your life doesn't start and stop. It continues throughout our entire life! It may slow and speed up throughout our lives because of life's events and challenges, but it continues, and you should push for more dreams at every age and stage of your life! So while you're busy planning goals, taking action on goals, persisting through the tough times of goal achievement, and even while you're achieving goals, you must also think about what is next in life. Your growth, experiences, and achievements allow you to grow further, and your dreams can take you there. I've found that many of my early dreams in life that resulted in goals being set in my twenties have been reached by the time I reached fifty years of age. So it's time to begin to dream again in various categories of life. If you find that you don't have the dreams you once had or choose to change the scope or size of your dreams, enjoy that too! There will be times in life at various stages and challenges that the dream you have is simply to get through your present stage or current crisis. That is okay, and instead of thinking five years into the future, you're now focusing on five months into the future or even the next month. Remember, keep looking forward. Don't look back, You're not alone, especially when God is providing you those God-driven dreams!

Chapter 3
The Goal-Setting Process

✓ *Dream Great Dreams by Letting God In!*
   Create an environment that allows you to pray and ask God what dreams you should set goals for. Make sure that you find a place and time when you can comfortably dream great dreams.

✓ *Dream Your Dreams by Category*
   By focusing on spiritual, physical and mental, educational, family and social, career, financial or adventure you can balance your life and your lifetime goals.

✓ *Evaluate Your Dreams*
   Once you've written your dreams down determine if these goals are lifetime, 2-4yr goals or annual goals. By writing them down, your dreams become goals!

✓ *Lifetime Goals*
   Those goals that cannot be accomplished this year or even in the next 2-4 years should be considered lifetime goals. These goals are special and will take considerable effort, time and investment to achieve . . . but worth it!

✓ *Two-Year to Four-Year Goals*
   Those goals that cannot be accomplished this year because of other things going on in your life, or you simply choose not to work on this goal for a few years becomes your 2-4yr goals.

✓ *Annual Goals*
   Those goals that can be achieved in one year become annual goals. They may not be finished this year depending on when you started them but if they can be started and finished in a 12-month timeline, they should be listed as your annual goals.

✓ *Monthly Goals*
   Those goals that can be started and achieved in relatively shorter time periods will become your monthly goals. These goals many times are sub-goals to larger goals you're planning to achieve.

- ✓ *Weekly Goals*
  These are usually the beginning of other goals but the first step may be the toughest in any worthy goal pursuit! Remember the saying, "a journey of ten thousand miles, begins with a single step."

- ✓ *The Twenty-Five LPI-Goal Achieving Techniques*
  Regardless of your goals being a weekly or lifetime goal, there are 25 techniques that you can use to accomplish your goals!

- ✓ *Dream More Dreams*
  The process of dreaming great dreams doesn't stop! It continues throughout a lifetime. Whatever age or stage you're in, whether you're pursuing a goal or just completed one, it is time to dream more dreams!

Chapter 4

THE FOUR STAGES OF GOAL ACHIEVEMENT

The process of goal achievement can be broken into many steps. After forty years of achieving meaningful goals, I have used a twenty-five-step process for goal achievement that I break into four stages. At this time, a simple introduction to each of the stages will be explained. The stages include the thinking or planning and mental stage, the action-oriented stage, the sluggishness-of-the-persistence stage, and the actual achievement stage. Each of the stages has several steps that we'll examine in the remaining chapters of this book. However, it should be noted that the planning stage has seven steps while the other three stages have six steps. This points out, simply, the importance of the planning and mental stage.

The Planning and Mental Stage: Plan It!

The first stage of goal achievement is to plan your goal! By now you have turned your dreams into goals by writing them down. While writing it down is one of the steps in this stage of planning it, there is much more thought that needs to go into how you're going to achieve a goal. In this stage, your mind is beginning to work through many aspects of why you want to achieve the goal as well as asking God why you should achieve it. At this stage, we want to understand the details of what it is that we're going to specifically achieve. To know that, we'll need to do some research and even determine if this is the best time in our life to accomplish this particular goal. Knowing when to talk openly about your goal and even when to share it with others is also part of the planning and mental stage.

The Action Stage: Making It Happen!

Once your goal is thought through and planned, the second stage is the action or "making it happen" stage. This stage is when the action begins! You will take steps monthly, weekly, daily, or even hourly toward achieving the goal! In order to assure that we're making things happen, we need to create measurements and action-oriented behavior that demonstrates to ourselves that we're moving toward goal achievement. When we find that we're making things happen, even if it is a very small accomplishment or slowly progressing, we should celebrate our movement, which is also one of the steps of this stage.

The Persistence Stage: Sticking to It!

One of the challenges of every goal is that there are going to be roadblocks, challenges, negative attitudes, or even an inability to stay focused on achieving your goal. The bigger the goal, the more roadblocks are bound to occur. This third stage is about sticking to with it even when others begin to doubt or even when you begin to doubt whether you are going to be able to achieve the goal! Realizing that this stage is going to occur, anticipating what may be between you and goal achievement, and even understanding techniques to get through it, are all vital toward your success of achieving your goal. Too many times this is the stage that stops goals from being achieved. However, whether our courage is lacking at times, the roadblocks are too big, or negative thinking overcomes us during this stage, we can stick to it and persist and achieve the goal by knowing six techniques at this stage!

The Achievement Stage: Achieving It!

The fourth stage of goal achievement is what I call the achievement stage! In this stage, while it sometimes comes quickly or immediately after the completion of the other three stages, it can also be drawn out for months or even years and even require techniques to help us to complete the goal. Sometimes we can find ourselves inches from the finish line of achievement, and we need that little push or incentive to accomplish the goal. But the process of achievement, how we receive it, and what happens next becomes important in goal-achieving success. Sometimes we find that by achieving one goal, we can actually accomplish another goal more easily. In this stage, we'll examine ways to cross the finish line and set our sights on the next race too!

Now let's begin to take a closer look at each of the stages and, more importantly, also begin to explore each of the twenty-five steps of goal achievement!

Chapter 4
Stages of Goal Achievement

✓ *The Planning and Mental Stage: Plan It!*
Whether the goal is a lifetime goal requiring years to prepare and achieve or an easy one month goal, the process of planning to achieve it and thinking through it happens at the beginning called the Planning and Mental Stage. This stage is crucial for the success of achievement.

✓ *The Action Stage: Making It Happen!*
This is the stage where you are beginning to move toward achievement! You need action, measurement and a bit of celebration when you notice that you're beginning to move closer to reaching goals.

✓ *The Persistence Stage: Sticking to It!*
Now that you're into the pursuit of achievement, the tough times surely come. Fear, doubt, roadblocks, fatigue all can set in and you've simply got to stick to it if your going to prevail. The persistence stage can last one day or for years depending on the goal being a lifetime goal or a monthly goal.

✓ *The Achievement Stage: Achieving It!*
In the achievement stage you're now focused on the "finish line" and even beginning to believe you're going to reach it. Sometimes however, incentives and that extra push can help at the end of pursuing your goals.

Chapter 5

Planning and Mental Stage: Plan It!

The most important part of the goal achievement is the planning and mental stage! This is the stage where things are created conceptually. This is the stage where God enters into your goals, and this is the stage where you firmly commit yourself toward achieving your goals! There are seven steps in the planning and mental stage of goals. These are, for the most part, mental exercises, but each step is vitally important to create the foundation of a goal that will be achieved in your lifetime! To begin, first think about why you want to achieve this objective. This stage is sometimes a bit of a reality check as well because you need to come to grips with what dreams you really want in your life and why you want to achieve them!

Pray It!

While the individual planning steps in this chapter can happen simultaneously or even in a different order, I believe the first step in planning a goal is to ask God into your plan. By taking minutes, days, or months to pray about your goal, I believe you can better prepare yourself to be mentally strong enough to overcome any challenge that comes your way in the pursuit of your goals. Just think, with God for you, who could possibly be against you?

Finding God in your lifetime plans, in the crisis of the day, in relationships with your spouse, parents, children, neighbors, bosses, and subordinates cannot be a bad thing—ever! Sometimes we want to create the goal and go after achieving it immediately. Take the time to stop and ask God why you should pursue this goal. Ask, "Lord, how can I glorify your name by achieving it?" Asking God for patience, knowledge, resources, and guidance is a wonderful way to live a life of abundance! When times get tough, and they will, and you think you may not be able to accomplish the goal, knowing that God was with you way back at the beginning of creating this goal can help you sustain any roadblocks or setbacks in the process.

Another technique in bringing God into your goal-planning stage is to actually create a prayer for your goal! Whether the goal is to get; the first job, the first date, the new job, buy your first house, or to fight illness, or survive life-threatening injuries or diseases, or simply passing the exam at the end of the week, I believe God is there for you and enjoys being part of your life! So create a specific prayer that you can come back to over and over throughout your pursuit of the goal. This can be something that you write down (I would recommend it) or something that you continue to pray as you pursue your goal. If others are helping you to achieve the goal, they too can use your prayer, and just think of the power of prayer if you had several people praying for you to achieve your goal.

Personalize It!

The next step in planning your goal is to personalize it! Why do you want to achieve the goal? What does it do for you personally, spiritually, emotionally, financially, physically, educationally? Do you want to achieve this goal for the right moral reasons? Do you want to accomplish this goal for yourself, or are you doing this because your wife or husband, parents or children, coworkers or boss wants you to? Are you trying to achieve the goal because everyone else is going for the same kind of goal, or are you are trying to impress someone else? By understanding the real reason you want to achieve your goal, you will establish a solid foundation toward achievement. In the tough times that come, you'll know that you're achieving the goal for the right reasons, and you will be able to maintain the stamina to overcome the critics that suggest that you're doing it for the money, fame, attention, or even for your ego. Ask yourself, "When I complete this goal, how will it help me to help others? How will achieving this goal help me to grow? Is the purpose that I want to reach this dream for the right reasons, and will it benefit either myself or others for the right reasons?" Know the real reason that you want to achieve your goal, and you will be on your way to achieving any goal that you set!

Clarify It!

All goals need to be clarified! Regardless of your age, your stage of life, or even the complexity of the goal, the more specific you can be about the goal, the more likely it is that you will achieve it! Along with our mental capacity of knowing exactly want we want, our prayers being very focused on what the goal is, by clarifying the goal, we will have a better chance of knowing when we achieve it! We will also have a better chance in knowing how to achieve and when to achieve it. If we are thinking about retirement and we are not sure of how much money we will need or how much money we will have available, it becomes difficult to know the amount you will need to set for a goal! If we know that we intend to travel four times a year to see the grandchildren and how much each trip will cost as well as the amount for monthly rental and food expenses and the like, we can begin to plan for obtaining the income to sustain this plan. If on the other hand, as another example, we feel that we want to learn about artistic expression but are not sure if it should be by painting or sculpting, chances are we'll have a hard time setting a goal to learn about any of them. If we know that we want to purchase the first house with a blue front porch, a white picket fence, a two-car garage, and four bedrooms, we're much closer than when we "want a new house." Clarify your goal down to details, and you're on your way toward achieving it! This may require that you do research before you can clarify it. We'll discuss the research shortly, but for now, know that identifying the details of your goal will help you to achieve it.

Write It!

One of the comments that I receive extensively is "Yes, I have goals, I just haven't written them down." This is, I believe, one of the major mistakes that can be made in *not* accomplishing goals! You need to write your goals down on paper, on a napkin, or even cardboard! Even typing your goals into a computer is better than not writing down your goals. By hand-writing goals down, it has been found that we have an exceedingly higher probability to achieve them than if we're walking around with goals only in our minds. Part of the reason is that by writing goals down, we are embedding the idea in our subconscious mind, and whether we are consciously thinking about it or not, our mind continues to figure out ways to gather the resources to reach the goal. If you haven't done this before, I would strongly suggest that you try it! Pick two ideas or goals that you want to focus on. Write one of the goals down and, as it was pointed out previously, make sure that you clarify it as you write it. Then simply think of the other goal. After a week, see which one gets more attention! You'll notice that the one that you clarified and wrote down continues to come to mind, and your thoughts will focus on ways to accomplish it. The fact is that we generally have way too many things going on to remember every thought that comes our way. So by writing the goals that you're serious about on paper and clarifying exactly what you want to accomplish, you can relieve yourself from trying to remember this goal and everything else you need to on a daily basis.

Now that we're going to write them down, the next question is, where should they be written? LPI provides a Life Achievement Planner that walks you through the entire process, from dreaming great dreams to writing goals for your lifetime goals, two—to four-year goals, annual goals, and even monthly goals. By writing your goals down, whether it is in a Life Achievement Planner (available at *www.lifeplannersnow.com*) or a notebook, you can save them for reference throughout your life and even share them with your children or grandchildren. You can show your children and grandchildren how you identified goals, and they can learn how to write their goals too! Imagine for a minute, if you want to pass something on to your children or grandchildren, can you think of a better life skill than being able to dream great dreams and then taking steps to achieve them?

Research It!

Now that the dream has moved to a written goal and is clarified, the work begins! To understand how to complete the degree, purchase the car, travel to Spain, raise money for the local Boy Scout troop, have the entire family go on a vacation to Florida, it all takes research. If you're going to run a marathon or lose twenty pounds, if you want to join a local church or visit several of the state parks, you're going to need to learn the extent and preparation that will be required to achieve these goals. Typically, once a goal is identified, we want to immediately begin to achieve it. In order to be successful, it is well-advised to take some time and think through the process and learn what you'll have to do to achieve your goal. Will you need to increase your discretionary income? Will you need to pursue additional education? Will you need to visit your doctor before starting an exercise program? Should you talk to a career counselor before pursuing a new career? The more you can think through and research the mountain that you want to climb, the easier your trek will be!

One aspect of pursuing big goals might be that you may need to create subgoals to achieve first. We will describe more thoroughly the process of subdividing your goals later in the action stage. For now, identify each goal that you've listed and determine what you will need to learn to prepare to achieve the goal or what training you will have to complete to reach your goal.

Without going negative on any goal or dream that you have, another piece of the research portion of goal setting is to identify potential roadblocks that may keep you from reaching your goal. Will the financial costs be too high? Will the physical toll or the mental stress be too great? Will you find that you may not receive any support from family or friends? Will you need to learn to speak publicly before you submit your name to run for public office? As part of the research you should identify anything that might be there that could trip you or derail your mission. Being able to anticipate those roadblocks in advance and then determine ways to bust through these setbacks will move you closer to achievement! Along with the roadblocks and how you might overcome them, list those initial steps that you will take to research your goals.

Time It!

An exciting step in the planning stage of goal setting is deciding when you will begin to pursue your goals and when you anticipate achieving them! This process should be thought through carefully as well. Some of the thoughts that you will need to consider come from the previous steps. The extent of research you do will help you to complete this step. If you've learned that you're going to need to complete a certification in order to be eligible for a job interview, this will surely affect your timeline in getting the job. Furthermore, if you know that you want to have your children join the local soccer league, which is only offered a few months of the year, you'll need to plan accordingly for the second and third quarters of the year, unless you're considering indoor soccer too!

Sometimes life gets too busy, or you just know that this isn't the time to pursue a goal. Don't worry. Rather, simply list your goal as a lifetime goal and list the beginning in the next few years rather than the next few months. The more realistic we can be about attempting to start or complete the goal in our time frame, the more successful we'll feel when we're in the middle of the pursuit. When I decided to list a goal to visit all the fifty states in the United States, I gave myself several years to achieve it. Knowing that life was crazy and I couldn't do this in the next few years, I made a goal to visit all fifty states by the time I was fifty! It worked, and I achieved this goal in about twenty years! So whether you are in your teens, in your twenties, in your thirties, or even in your sixties, determine if this is the right time to start or to complete your goal. Allow for life to get in the way, but definitely, set a timeline to accomplish. And then if necessary, give yourself a break, and if you don't achieve it on your timeline, realize that God has his timeline when he wants you to achieve it, and be patient—you will get there!

Secure It!

Another important step when we're thinking about goals is when to keep it to yourself and when to share your goals with others. When I was in junior high school, I made a goal that I kept to myself for a few years. The goal was to be the senior speaker at my high school graduation. The school that I attended allowed for the speakers to be chosen by a contest. Some high schools give this opportunity to their valedictorian or salutatorian, but my high school wanted to allow students to compete for it. So I decided while in middle school that I wanted to be that speaker at graduation. As we either know or remember, sharing dreams or goals with classmates while in middle school or high school could result in being laughed at, and we then cave in to peer pressure rather than pursuing what we truly want to achieve. So for three years I didn't tell anyone, not even my brothers. Each year, because I was in the band, I would attend the graduation exercises and listened intently to the speeches, and each year I moved closer toward my goal by knowing what my speech should sound like. During my senior year, the time came for the contest and competition. I knew that when it became known that I was competing, some of my closest friends would be supportive, but I also knew that some of my closest friends would find it quite funny to see me trying out for this contest. Two observations that I learned at this age were that you can anticipate those close to you to challenge your talent, your intent, and your chances of accomplishing any kind of a goal. The second observation was I knew the ridicule would come, and frankly knowing this, I used it as a motivator toward achieving my goal. I figured I would be fully prepared to win the contest and show them! It worked! And on June 6, 1979, I gave a speech to my graduating class of more than six hundred students and with an estimated crowd of four thousand to six thousand in attendance in the Memorial Coliseum in Fort Wayne, Indiana.

There have been several examples in life for me, and I'm sure for you too where you told someone a goal and found either support or something less than that! Don't forget that if you included God into your dreams during the dream stage, who could possibly be against you? That said, it is important to realize that the timing of when you want to tell someone about your goal can work for you or against you.

Other times in my life, I have made a goal public in front of others, knowing that once I made it public, I would be forced to pursue it and not turn back it. Along with an internal commitment, by sharing with others, you may create a support network to assist you in achieving your goal. Some examples of needing a support network could include if you're planning to lose fifty pounds or if you are unemployed and looking for a job, or planning to stop smoking or having to fight cancer, you will need those around you to help you reach your goal. By sharing your goal, you can find that much-needed support from those around you!

So whether you anticipate positive or negative reaction once you make your goal public, make sure that you've done your research on what will be expected of you, and by knowing the sacrifice required, you will be able to stand firm should you find those around you less than supportive.

Chapter 5
Planning Mental Stage: Planning It!

- ✓ *Pray It!*
  The first step of setting goals is to pray about it and ask God if this goal is something that you should pursue. Knowing that God is with you in your goal will help you "move mountains!"

- ✓ *Personalize It!*
  Is this goal your goal? Do you want to accomplish it for you? Do you want to achieve it for the right reasons? When you achieve this goal how will it help you or others?

- ✓ *Clarify It!*
  To achieve your goal, you must know exactly what it is that you want to accomplish. Have you specified the details of your goal? Do you know when you plan to reach your goal? By clarifying your goal, you give your mind the opportunity to determine how you're going to get there . . . so clarify it today!

- ✓ *Write It!*
  Once you know the details in mind about the dream you have, you need to write it down. Once written, your dream becomes a goal! By writing the goal down, you join an exclusive club because it's been estimated that less than 5% of those who set goals actually write them down. Those that write them down achieve them while others only dream about them.

- ✓ *Research It!*
  To know the sacrifice, financial commitment, emotional stress, the education or support from the family that will be required, you will have to research how to reach your goal. Take the time during the planning and mental stage to fully understand what will be required from you to achieve your goal.

- ✓ *Time It!*
  Goals can be started at anytime of your life. Is this the best time for you to start to pursue your goal? Are the other commitments in life going to allow you the time necessary for your success?

Remember it has been said, "That there are two best times to plant an oak tree. The first time is twenty years ago. The second best time is today!" So if you haven't yet started those lifetime goals…maybe now is the time!

✓ *Secure It!*
Sometimes, telling others should wait until you've researched or fully thought through your commitment of your goal. Sometimes, on the other hand, by sharing your goal with others, you can find that they will encourage and support you to pursue and achieve your goal!

Chapter 6

Action Stage: Making It Happen!

The planning and mental stage can last an hour or years. Whether you've spent an hour of time or several years thinking about your goal, the action stage can't come soon enough if you are excited about getting on with accomplishing your goals! This is the stage where things begin to happen.

First, however, is that one of the dangers in the goal-setting process happens when you've allowed too much time to elapse before you start making something happen. Sometimes negative thoughts can overcome your idea. Sometimes you doubt yourself and your idea, and you begin to feel that you're never going to achieve this goal. "It's too big or too overwhelming for me!" So keep in mind, if you've worked through the planning and mental stage and you've watched time slip away without starting on your goal, you may begin to lose hope that you will actually complete this goal. To overcome this feeling, you've got to get moving! There are six steps in the action stage and we will begin with subdividing your goal.

Subdividing Your Goal

One of the reasons that millions of people walk around with goals only in their mind is because they perceive the goal to be too big to pursue! They want the big house, they want a four-year degree, they want to eliminate ten credit cards and $50,000 in debt, they want to change their jobs or careers, or they want to lose one hundred pounds, or become a millionaire, or travel the world or even live in Hawaii. These goals are examples of goals that could easily be broken into smaller ones.

I would suggest that if a goal is to take more than a year or a considerable amount of financial commitment or physical challenge, you will need to break your goal into smaller parts or, as some refer to them, as milestones. While you can leave the overall goal on a lifetime-goal chart, you may want to create annual or two to four goals as sub-goals that you can begin to work on now toward the bigger goal.

Throughout my adult life, I have had times when I've really wanted to get healthy. Each time that I set a goal to become healthier, I find that I need to break my goals into smaller objectives. When I wanted to lose twenty-five pounds, I first had to set the goal to begin to exercise and eat better. Even before I set the dietary goal of eating better, I thought I would first have to eliminate the daily intake of two cans of soda. So I began to eliminate the two cans of pop down to one can. Then I decided I was going to run to lose weight. I love running! However, before I could start running, I would have to walk for several weeks to get my knees and heart in better shape. Over time, my body began to want more exercise. So I jumped on the elliptical trainer and bike. As my exercise routine began to grow, I felt my appetite began to shrink, and I could eat less. So after a one-year regimen (with various injuries) and several subgoals, I began to reach my goal of losing twenty-five pounds. When I first set the goal of losing twenty-five pounds, I frankly thought, *I haven't weighed my goal weight for twenty years! How will I ever get back to that weight?* But by breaking down the goal to smaller steps or milestones, it became more realistic, and psychologically, it became easier to achieve as well.

If you're finding that you are *not* moving because it just seems too big of a goal to achieve, try to subdivide your goals to make them more realistic to accomplish.

Movement

Now that you have thought through your goals, you're now ready to make something happen. In fact, in this step, you have to take action to know that something is happening! To be a little more precise, if you feel that you are not making progress toward achieving your goal, you will begin to doubt your ability to obtain it. Let's look at an example of a learning adventure goal of gardening. In order to begin to achieve a goal of gardening, several steps come to mind. These steps include reading and learning about this subject. It also includes determining where you will plant your garden. Another step is deciding what you are going to plant and when do you begin to plant your garden to name only a few of the steps. To make sure that you're moving toward your goal, you have to have movement. Therefore, you should create a list of steps that will demonstrate to yourself that you are moving toward your objective. These steps could be as simple as the following:

1. Buy a book on gardening, visit a library to find a book on gardening or Google it to learn more.
2. Read the book or article on gardening.
3. Determine where the garden will be.
4. Decide on what will be planted in it.
5. Determine when you will begin to plant what you've decided to plant.

By listing these steps, you can easily identify when and how you are making things happen. From the list above, you can also add dates to each task to make sure that you reach your goal on schedule or, in this case, you don't miss the planting season!

Without having some outline or list that you can review, you won't know if you are effectively moving toward your goals. So create a checklist that will show that you are making progress toward achieving your goals. This will build confidence in yourself toward the pursuit of achievement.

Daily Review

We've all heard the comment "Out of sight, out of mind." This technique of reviewing your goal daily simply keeps the goal and your objective to achieve it in front of you so that you keep thinking about it and keep taking action to achieve it. To be sure that you are moving toward your goals, you must be able to see movement, but in order to see the movement, you must review your progress daily! If you're serious about reading the Bible this year, determining what you've read already and what you need to read next are great strategies to do daily. These days, there are more than enough electronic aids, including the iPhones, iPads, e-readers, and computers to name only a few, that can assist in these daily reviews.

Visual Steps

The visual steps technique is when you create something visually that can show what steps you need to do to achieve your goals. Whereas the measure it step, to be discussed next, has some aspects of visual aids, this step more concretely suggests that you use a calendar, develop a chart showing each of the steps, show a graph demonstrating your weight each week for six months, or even use LPI's Life Achievement Planner that can help by visually showing next steps you need to take during the month. Making a picture of the steps you must achieve daily, weekly, monthly, or quarterly can keep you focused on movement and demonstrate visually to you that you are moving closer to your goal. So if the family is planning the long-awaited vacation to Aspen, Colorado, you might show the goal on a calendar and, each month or weekly, show what steps have to be taken to secure a successful trip. This technique, while not rocket science, is vitally important as another tool to take action and show visually your progress in achieving your goals.

Measurement

What gets measured gets done! So measure every step of the process. If you are going to accomplish anything in life, you're going to need to measure your achievement. Those smaller steps or milestones can help to create a measurement, but even if you don't have milestones, you still need to determine a way to effectively measure your progress.

As you're thinking about goals in the areas of finance, physical and mental health, education, or many of the adventure goals, you will be able to easily determine what to measure and how to measure progress. So whether it's to increase biking by thirty minutes a day or to increase income or reduce debt, whether it is to learn how to play chess or visit all the zoos in your state, or to paint your house this next summer you can track the progress made toward your goal. If you want to read a book or study class notes to pass a test or use the research material that you purchased in preparation for an exam, the books you read or the time you prepare for the exam, all can be measured to show that you're making progress toward achieving your goal, which is to pass the test.

The more difficult goals to measure may include goals such as spiritual, career, family or social, or adventure goals that focus on experiences. These areas could include developing a more meaningful relationship with your husband or wife or, if you're single, creating a more meaningful relationship with a significant boyfriend or girlfriend. If you want to experience peace or joy, become more happy or compassionate in your life, forgive more or learn to be more generous, you will need to think through ways that you can measure your progress. If your goal is to laugh more next month or next year, how do you intend to measure this goal? Each of these areas or any goal, whether tangible or intangible, can be measured. It just takes a bit more effort to effectively measure your intangible goals. If your goal is to raise your self-esteem or the self-esteem of a close friend, how would you measure this goal? You could consider both the input and the effort that you put into the process to accomplish the goal (the books you read or the counseling sessions you attend), or you could focus outcomes or behavior exhibited (the individual is happier with themselves and demonstrates more positive behavior publicly, counting the good days and/or events occurring).

Virtually everything that you want to obtain, achieve, or complete can be measured, so take some time and decide on what should be measured so that you can see that you're making progress toward achieving your goal. If you find that progress isn't occurring, it may mean that you break down the steps further to make progress easier.

Celebration

The time comes when a milestone or sub-goal or even the goal is completed! Even when the smallest steps of progress are made, it is vitally important to celebrate it! If the results of the test come back and your health has improved or it hasn't gotten worse, celebrate it! When you study two hours for the exam or simply buy the travel guide to explore destinations for a trip with your spouse in five years, reward yourself for taking the first step!

I believe that goals are fun to identify, set, and especially achieve. So to keep both a balance of goals to be achieved in the future as well as enjoying the pursuit of the goals you're working on today, you will need to decide how you will celebrate your achievements. Celebrating your first steps is different than creating incentives, which we'll discuss later. Celebrating is a mental state in which you simply give yourself a break! It isn't necessarily buying yourself a gift. It has more to do with you rewarding yourself with excitement, peace, contentment, happiness, joy, or even relaxation. Although it can be an opportunity to buy yourself a gift, it just isn't a preplanned gift. Rather, after the kids completed a year of school, once you finished the race, after you reached your fund-raising goal, after you hired the new member of your sales team, stop and take a moment to celebrate it! Take a couple of days off once you've reached a milestone before you start again the pursuit of the goal. Enjoy a dinner with the entire family once they are able to travel to meet each other after several years. Many times the pursuit of goals can be stressful and mentally challenging. This is the time in which you let go and enjoy the moment. Even if you're pursuing building a house and you've finally come to an agreement on the design and layout celebrate it. There will be many more challenges in the pursuit of meaningful goals. So take a minute, a breather, a weekend, or whatever the case and celebrate the moment before going further in the goal-achievement process or beginning to pursue another goal.

I've found that the opportunity to reflect upon the progress that was made becomes mentally crucial, particularly if it is a stressful goal that was being pursued. But knowing that God was with you at the beginning and continues to be with you at the completion of the milestone or after you've reached your goals, why not thank God and have him as part of your celebration too!

Chapter 6
Action Stage: Making It Happen!

✓ *Subdividing your Goal*
Sometimes goals are so big, that we need to break them into smaller ones (sometimes called milestones) to help us move toward achievement. If the goal is too monumental or might take too long to achieve, or take too much commitment currently, break it into smaller steps so that you're moving toward success.

✓ *Movement*
The movement technique is to create ways to show conceptually or literally that you are moving toward your goal and moving toward achievement. Create charts, graphs, check-off lists to demonstrate movement toward your objectives so you can see your progress!

✓ *Daily Review*
Keeping your goal in front of you with notes on the bathroom mirror, in your car, on your iphone, on the refrigerator will help keep you focused on action toward reaching your goal. By reading and reviewing your progress as well as what is in front of you to overcome, you will continually evaluate ways to get there.

✓ *Visual Steps*
The visual steps technique is when you create something visually that can show what steps you need to do to achieve your goals.

✓ *Measurement*
What gets measured gets done! So measure every step of the process. If you are going to accomplish anything in life, you're going to need to measure your achievement.

✓ *Celebration*
The time comes when a milestone or sub-goal or even the goal is completed! Even when the smallest steps of progress are made, it is vitally important to celebrate it!

Chapter 7

PERSISTENCE STAGE: STICKING TO IT!

Nothing is final until you decide it is final! Goals are amazing things that we humans create. It's been said that only humans have the ability to visualize into the future. We can see the house, the bridge, the building, the town. We can create the colors and the beauty in our minds before we even begin the slightest effort in making it happen. No other creation on the planet can do that—just us! This obviously, I believe, is a God-given ability. By not taking full advantage of visualizing and fully utilizing our minds through the creation and completion of a goal, we're missing out on the beauty of life and living life abundantly!

The persistence stage is the mental-workout stage of goal achievement. While we have the ability to see in our minds the goal to be achieved (which we'll discuss in a moment), we also have the mental capability of derailing or convincing ourselves to give up or give in when the pursuit becomes tough. So knowing what steps to take to mentally persevere; when you're faced with a letter that states you're on academic probation while in college or you damage the cartilage in your knee while training for the marathon or you're told you didn't make the cut this year in the tryouts for the basketball team or were turned down to be in the school play or even the boy or girl turns you down when you ask them out on a date, is crucial in the persistence stage. The list goes on and on for sure. We know that there have been millions of examples of man overcoming challenges at all stages of life for everything you can think of. Therefore, we must also know and have faith that we can and will overcome all odds when wanting to achieve our goals. The only impossibility lies within us. If we eliminate the "not possible" mentality from our vocabulary and our mental focus, with God's help we can then accomplish the impossible!

Think about a goal that you've wanted to achieve and didn't. Many times if we get to the root of why we did not achieve it, you can find it was this persistence stage that tripped us up! Books have been written however, on examples of individuals either not giving up or even after they failed numerous times, they continued until they were successful. This happened because they were able to persist and make it through this stage.

I've spent a good portion of my life teaching my children what my father taught me—that the glass is half full! I do think this stage is about a mental obstacle course, and having a positive mind-set will help to get you through it. Do you have to be raised an optimist to persevere? No, but it sure helps! Let's begin to review each of the steps of this stage, but remember, many times in pursuing our goals it will take every step in this stage to continue to reach our goal. Sometimes, you'll be able to move through this stage with relative ease. Knowing that this stage is however inevitable when achieving goals, you can better prepare and use the techniques listed to help you move toward the achievement of your goals.

Obstacles and Roadblocks

When dreaming your dreams and writing your goals, the one thing you can count on is the obstacles and roadblocks that will assuredly come your way! Anticipating and preparing for potential or expected roadblocks is crucial and can be fun for the success of your pursuit. If you didn't think through the possible roadblocks in advance during the planning stage of goal setting, then you're going to deal with it now as you're pursuing it.

Anything worth pursuing in life will have obstacles and roadblocks to confront before achieving it. To move these roadblocks and obstacles from a mental challenge to a strategy to overcome, you need to write them down and recognize them for what they are! If you're short on money to take the vacation, if your job was eliminated putting you on the street, if your spouse leaves you, if you're born into a family of crime, if the tornado levels your entire home in ruins and everything you own and have obtained in life is lost, if the car accident results in the amputation of your legs, or in a smaller sense, you didn't pass the test, you didn't get the job, or you didn't get the date, whatever the situation that comes at you, realize that the roadblocks in life are *not* permanent!

Think about the actual roadblock we encounter on the highway. When we set out to drive anywhere and encounter a roadblock, we don't go back home and decide to sell the car! In order to get through a roadblock, however, we sometimes are required to slow down before we can go through it. We sometimes even come to a stop while the construction crew finishes and then moves, and then traffic begins to slowly pick up speed again. Eventually, we go through the roadblock though at a bit slower pace or even possibly delayed to our destination, but we get through it! Sometimes we're even required to take the detour to another side road completely going around the construction area. Or sometimes we wait until the construction is completed and they allow traffic to resume. Roadblocks are not permanent! They delay us, they require us to wait until something changes, or they require that we take a different route! But they are not permanent!

So whatever you experience in life that delays your goal achievement, those roadblocks that slow us down or that may simply require us to wait or those roadblocks that require we take a different path, all allow us to keep pursuing our goals! If we are persistent, roadblocks are not permanent! The trick is to anticipate them. If you know that you're pursuing a goal that will take several months or even years to achieve, count on life to get in the way. Roadblocks in life come in all sizes and levels of challenge. Whether you're short on finances or have been told by experts that you don't have the skill, talent, funding, knowledge, or ambition, don't let others determine your destiny! You decide if this is simply a roadblock and then determine if you should wait, go at a slower pace, or change your direction to achieve your goals!

TDD for Achievement: Tenacity, Drive, and Determination

Along with roadblocks, another factor that will affect your ability to persist in achieving your goals is your ability to demonstrate tenacity, drive, and determination.

One of the things I find interesting in personalities is the level of pain and anguish each is able to sustain whatever the reason. Some are able to take on enormous amounts of trials in life, and those of us around them wonder how they do it. Others seem to collapse at smaller challenges of life. We've heard the saying "God only gives us as much as we can handle," and it does seem to have merit. This mind-set has even more importance if you have included God into your dreams and goals of life! If you know that God is there and remains there as you pursue your goals, you also know that he'll only allow as much challenge as he knows you can handle. If we look at the definition of these three goal-achieving traits, they include the following:

Tenacity—Ability to remain firm and steadfast over time
Drive—Ability to motivate, initiate and be ambitious
Determination—Ability to remain strong, demonstrate willpower and grit

We can easily see that we need each of these behaviors particularly as the goals get bigger in life! Think about any of the goals that you have in life presently in any of the areas of goals we've previously covered, from spiritual goals, physical and mental goals, educational goals, family and social goals, financial goals, career goals, or any of the adventure goals that you may be currently pursuing. To have achieved any of your lifetime goals or if you've already achieved other significant goals, you had to demonstrate tenacity, drive and determination.

One of the bigger and arguably the most important goals in life is raising children. The idea that when we're holding our child for the first time in life and undoubtedly embarking on a goal that will last at least twenty years is more than most of us could comprehend, especially at the time the baby lands in our arms! So those of you that might be wondering what goals should be set or if you feel that you haven't had any meaningful goals in life, think again because your ability to raise children requires all three of those traits of determination, drive, and tenacity. There will be good times, difficult and trying times, and even times when, both as parents and at times as children, we let the other down. Having the ability to get through a crisis or a time when life seems impossible, with TDD, we are able to carry on even when we think we can't. You may be at one of those times in your life now as you're raising children, and what better goal to set than to think about how to grow your family closer together, grow with your children, and grow as a parent! So remember that as goals are bigger and take longer to achieve, such as raising your children and family, your level of tenacity, drive, and determination will be challenged! We all have levels of tenacity, drive, and determination, and we will have just enough to get us through those God-driven dreams!

Staying Focused

Along with being challenged with TDD for those big goals in life, we will assuredly be challenged further in staying focused too. One of the amazing aspects of living life abundantly is that we'll at times feel that the commitments, appointments, demands, and challenges of life can overwhelm us! The goal-achieving technique of staying focused recognizes that among everything else in life, we can still focus on the goals that will help us live life abundantly. Living a bigger and more abundant life will assuredly challenge us to stay focused on the important goals of life. By using the Life Achievement Planner (available at www.lifeplannersnow.com) annually, you can keep focused on both short-term goals and lifetime goals too.

I like running. It has been and continues to be a goal in my life to run a marathon. I started running in my twenties and I have been able to run in several minimarathons in my adult life. These goals of running minimarathons were achieved even after a broken leg resulting in a plate and five screws in my knee. For this reason the minimarathons (13.1 miles) that I like to run are all flat courses. This is because my body prefers flat courses. What I've noticed particularly, because my knees can sometimes work against me, is that when I'm confronted with a hill of any kind (I refer to any incline as a hill as I am from northern Indiana and have grown accustomed to flatness when running!), I know that my focus needs to close in considerably. Instead of looking into the distance when I'm running uphill, I simply look down and focus on each step and think specifically about each step so that my knees don't get injured while running uphill!

When we're at the beginning or middle of a big goal, to keep focused, we sometimes need to focus on those daily steps and watch how we're pursuing the milestones or subgoals. If we lose focus on the small steps that are needed, we can easily lose focus on the overall goal too. With numerous demands for our time, various challenges in life, including our careers, the health issues of our children or parents or even ourselves, we can lose sight of what our lifetime goals are. So focus on the daily or weekly actions, or what you want to accomplish this month rather than "how steep or big the hill is." By focusing on the smaller steps when we pursue big goals, we can continue to move toward achievement while meeting the other demands that are continual in life.

Visualizing Success

When the pursuit of the goal is tough and the goal seems far from reachable, one technique that I've used successfully is to visualize your success in achieving the goal. The process of visualizing success can happen both mentally but can also be done by literal pictures of the achievement.

One of the goals I've had for thirty years was to run for and be elected to public office. The process of getting elected can be lengthy and stressful. In my case, it turned out to be about fourteen months from my decision to run until the actual general election . . . the second time! The first time I ran for office I lost by a slim margin. The next time had to wait sixteen years. In the second attempt, I was required to do hundreds of presentations, personal appearances, and knocking on hundreds of doors and visiting nearly two thousand homes over a fourteen-month period. During this goal, all the usual negative emotions, fears, life challenges entered into the process. One technique that I used that helped me get through this persistence stage was the ability to visualize success. I knew that on election night one of the traditions was to stand up and speak to the entire political party structure in the County. So early in the campaign season, I began to visualize standing up front and giving this victory speech. Many times throughout the campaign, when doubts would come to mind or negative comments would be told to me by friends, associates, or even strangers that were voting against me, I would simply see the vision of me giving the speech. It helped me to remain optimistic toward achieving this goal. I've used this visualization technique many times for hundreds of goals in my life, and it will work for you too!

Beyond the mental visioning lies an even more exciting process to visualizing your success, which is to actually take a picture of your success! This step, while requiring sometimes a bit of creativity, is well worth the result. If you see yourself owning a car, why not take a picture with it before you own it! If you know that your graduation in two years will be held at a certain location, borrow someone's cap and gown and have them take your picture at the location! If you know that you're going to live in a state, town, or neighborhood someday, have your picture taken there before you move in! If you want to lose weight, Photoshop a picture and see the result before you've achieved it! The idea is to give your mind a visual sense and an affirmation that you will achieve this goal—whatever the goal!

With today's ability to grab fast pictures from our phones, take pictures that you can hang up at home or post for you to see (remember, you may not want to go public on your goal yet) you can and should consider creating a visual of completing your goal. By putting pictures by your bed at night to review before going to sleep or putting pictures on your mirror in the bathroom or carrying pictures with you in your datebook or simply having them on your handheld devices, you are conditioning your mind for achievement of your goal. Create a vision of you finishing the race, accepting the diploma, having rice thrown at you at your wedding, having the first commission check handed to you, christening your first sailboat, simply being content and happy, completing the writing of your first book, or playing with your first puppy! Whatever your goal, see it and then believe it!

Experiencing It

Another technique is to experience the goal before you achieve it! So while this is a step further than the previous technique, taking a picture of it, to experience it, you actually try to go to the location or set the environment to match what you will experience once you reach your goal. This too can require some creativity but can make the pursuit fun and exciting too! One of the goals that I've listed for a lifetime goal is to go skydiving. Knowing that I was nearing the time that I would achieve this goal in life (I first had to lose twenty-five pounds to be eligible to sign up, and I had lost twenty pounds), I decided to first set a goal to complete indoor skydiving. By accomplishing this subgoal, I would not only get a picture of what it would be like (they would literally take a picture of me floating in the air), but I would also gain a perspective of what it would feel like and be like to go skydiving. So while traveling on a business trip in Orlando late one night after work, I purchased a ticket for an experience that was really cool! By going indoor skydiving, it prepared me for the bigger goal by literally giving me an experience of what it would feel like. By the way, by experiencing a goal mentally before you actually achieve it, you can even plan more effectively the emotional response you choose to have when you reach it. In this case, I know that I will be less nervous in the jump and be able to fully enjoy skydiving later this year! Now I only have to lose five more pounds to do it!

So if you want to experience finishing the race, walk the course and cross the finish line the day before the race begins! If you want to work at a company, arrive a day in advance of the interview and park in the parking lot to experience what you will ultimately feel like when you're hired. As my family began to grow, my wife and I knew that our kids would be going to schools that would be different from the area that our church was in. We made a goal that in the future we would move to another church. So one Sunday, my oldest son (nine years old at the time) and I visited a church that we had made a goal to attend, and we sat in the back pew to experience what it would be like to attend there. By experiencing the goal and what it might be like even before we made the official change, we knew what it might be like and how we would feel once we accomplished the goal.

By experiencing an event before it occurs or by going to a specific location (running on the football field and looking up to the bleachers before the tryouts begin) where you intend to complete a goal or actually conduct the act of achieving the goal, we set the tone mentally that we will achieve it and reduce or eliminate any negative notion that we may not reach our goals. Think about your goals and create the scenario to experience the goal before you actually achieve it!

Positive Mind-Set

Having read positive mental attitude books for forty years, I have learned that one of the most important persistence techniques in accomplishing your goals is to remain positive! Having a positive mind-set doesn't just happen. Rather, life has a tendency to throw negative attitudes, comments, and beliefs at you. So you need to create ways to keep thinking positive. If you're not planting seeds, you're bound to have weeds! So whether you're pursuing a goal or several goals, you should be planting positive mental attitude ideas on how you will be achieving them. Keep thinking positively until you've reached your goal!

There are several ways you can utilize this technique of creating a positive mind-set to help you achieve your goals. The list of ideas below identify ways that you can plant seeds and remain positive during the persistence stage of goal achievement. Pick at least one or several, or even better, use all of them!

Pray daily. By keeping God in your goal life, you can remain positive for your individual goal or all the goals that you are pursuing if you pray continually. As was mentioned previously, create a specific prayer just for your goal! Memorize it and pray it daily! Along with praying for your goal, there might even be other things that you could pray for too.

Read books and magazines. Find positive mental attitude articles and stories and keep reading them to stay positive. Read positive-thinking books, magazines, websites, and Facebook pages that are focused on positive messages. From authors such as Dyer, Waitley, Tracy, Zigler, Mackay, Osteen, Robbins, Maxwell, Schuller, Warren, Meyer, you can find these and many others for consideration for positive-living messages in hard copy, audiobooks, and even e-books.

Use CDs and online information. Listening to successful living messages or to motivational speakers and subscribing to daily messages or quotations online can keep you thinking positive too. YouTube provides numerous examples and material that are motivational and inspirational.

Exercise regularly. It's been proven that exercise it tied to remaining positive. By exercising, you keep those endorphins pumping in your mind and then your thoughts will remain optimistic. So, plan to exercise regularly.

Listen to music. By listening to positive music, you can keep your attitude upbeat throughout your pursuit of your goals. From Christian music, classical, country, rap, whatever the music that helps you remain positive, keep it coming to you throughout the day. I've volunteered to play drums in a praise band for my church which helps to have beautiful music coming to me in life. At one of the tough times in life, while feeling a bit down, my wife won tickets to a Matt Maher concert, and the music more than lifted my spirits. It rejuvenated my life! I purchased three of his CDs that night and had them in my home stereo system, my car, my laptop computer, my Ipad, and my iPhone! So at any time, I can listen to music that can lift my spirit!

Experience nature. For many of us, by experiencing nature, we can greatly improve our attitude positively as well. Walks in the park, hiking, listening to wind or birds can be inspiring for many and allow you to think positive and remain hopeful regardless of the challenges that you are pursuing. Nature has always seemed to put life in perspective, and it's free, continual, and everywhere you go!

Create a daily affirmation. By creating a simple saying, sentence, or thought about how you will achieve your goal, you can remain positive throughout the persistence stage of goal achievement. Bible verses could provide many positive affirmations too, including, "This is the day the Lord has made, and I will rejoice and be glad in it."

While conducting leadership training for a group of business leaders, I challenged them as a group to come up with a daily affirmation that can help them through the tough times in leading others. I was amazed when this group of twenty middle and senior managers, together as a group, selected "I can do all things through Christ who strengthens me" as a daily affirmation.

So whether you select a Bible verse or create a sentence that is meaningful to you, make sure that you have a positive, affirming statement about yourself or the goal at hand. "Today, I am one day closer to my fishing trip with my son!" Or "As the sun shines today, I know that I am growing into a more positive role model for my family!" Or "If I can see it, I will achieve it!" Yep, those rhyming sentences are fun and easy to remember, so get creative.

Once created, have it as a screen saver, put it on your phone, datebook, car, anywhere you can think to put it to remain positive toward achieving your goal!

Giving of yourself.

Have you ever noticed that it is better to give than to receive? If you're finding that you are not feeling positive, possibly down, disheartened, unhappy, or maybe even depressed at times in life, try setting a goal to help someone else! It is fascinating that when we spend less time focused on ourselves and begin to think of how to help someone else, we begin to feel better about our own situation! So another way to remain positive is to work at a food bank, take clothes to Goodwill, help on a mission project at your church, volunteer for your children's school project, or even simply take cookies to your neighbor. However you can focus on helping someone else, you will find it can be a huge step toward you remaining positive.

Why not create a list of ten ways you can help others so when in the midst of you pursuing your goals and you have difficulties, you already have identified ways to focus on others, and as a result, you can help them and yourself feel better. (This by the way can be a social goal or an experiencing goal too!)

Impactful weather.

One final thought in regards to maintaining a positive mind-set, while this doesn't fit into a goal-achieving step to take per se, be aware that there is enough evidence showing that both the weather and even the full moons can impact how we are feeling overall.

If we know that we must remain positive as we pursue our goals, we must also remember that high-pressure systems, including sunny weather, can improve our moods while low-pressure or cloudy, overcast weather can lower our moods. Simply be aware that the changes in climate and weather can impact us. The good news is that while we cannot change the weather, we can wait it out, and (in Indiana at least) it can and does change quickly.

Studies have also been conducted showing that there are reactions for some when they experience full moons. In fact, large metropolitan areas even increase staffing of their police department staffs and hospital emergency rooms when the calendar indicates a full moon. As a human resources professional for twenty years, I too have noticed people's reactions to the effects of a full moon on employees. So remember that the full moon can affect some people's personality too and, in the course of pursuing goals, could impact our ability to remain positive. The good news is that the full moon and high tide changes occur frequently, and we can wait these out too!

Chapter 7
Persistence Stage: Sticking to It!

✓ *Obstacles and Roadblocks*
Anything worth pursuing in life will have obstacles and roadblocks to confront before achieving it. To move these roadblocks and obstacles from a mental challenge to a strategy to overcome, you need to write them down and recognize them for what they are!

✓ *TDD for Achievement: Tenacity, Drive and Determination*
Having the ability to remain firm and steadfast over time, the ability to motivate, initiate and be ambitious and having the ability to remain strong, demonstrate willpower and grit are all indications of TDD and will keep you on course when faced with the persistence stage.

✓ *Staying Focused*
The goal-achieving technique of staying focused recognizes that there are many other aspects of life occurring while we pursue goals. Therefore, by reviewing our goals regularly, recognizing those roadblocks that are in front of us and knowing how much determination will be required helps us to stay focused on achieving our goals.

✓ *Visualize Success*
By either mentally imagining your success or actually taking pictures of your success before you achieve it, (taking an actual picture of you crossing the finish line before the race is started) can help you continually visualize your success.

✓ *Experience It*
Getting creative by going to the location of where you will achieve the goal and acting as you have already reached your goal . . . can set the mental image that you can and will accomplish your goal!

- *Positive Mindset*
  By praying, reading positive mental attitude books and magazines, listening to upbeat and motivational speeches or music, you can continue to feed your mind the energy that is required to see your goal through to completion.

Chapter 8

ACHIEVEMENT STAGE: ACHIEVING IT!

The process of achieving can come quickly, or it can come after years of pursuing your goal or goals. This chapter examines some steps to get us from the pursuing to achieving stage. Many times, particularly for goals that are big and take years to achieve, we may need that little extra something that helps us to complete the goal.

Before we review these techniques to achieve, let's first talk about the process of achievement. During this quick moment of "getting there," or a period of time when you're either nearing the completion or in the process of achievement, you need to realize that you're going to achieve the goal! By mentally preparing yourself toward achievement, you're creating the environment for success. Enjoy this moment whether it's sudden or over a period of time.

If on the other hand you're almost there and just can't seem to close the deal, pass the test, raise enough funds, lose those final five pounds, finish running the race, commit to joining a church, plan the family vacation, or ask the guy or girl out on a date, this chapter explores some techniques that can work at helping you over the hurdles of goal achievement.

Overshooting Your Goal

Sometimes in the process of goal achievement, we can get fixated on not being able to overcome the challenges of reaching our goals, or we seem to lose the drive at the final stages that will help us to accomplish our goal. I have watched this happen with individuals that seem to think that they aren't good enough to complete the goal. We have also seen examples where individuals, after a long pursuit lasting months or years, are at the final step and they somehow seem to have sabotaged their success by behaving in a way that eliminates their chances of completing their goal. Sometimes success in itself, especially after pursuing it for years, can be something we're scared of, or we may even wonder if we're worthy of it! If we have been fighting to achieve a goal for many years, we may begin to think that we're simply not supposed to reach it. Otherwise, if we were to achieve it, it should have been easy, and we should have accomplished it years ago.

If these thoughts have come to mind or you are almost there but need a little extra push to accomplish your objective, challenge yourself to establish a goal to overshoot your initial goal! While that may seem crazy (and it may be), we're training our minds to actually look beyond where we want to arrive.

One example was when I was trying to complete a certification exam that I needed to score at least 75 points to pass. I kept coming up just short of this number. At one attempt, I received a score of 72 and 69 at another. I kept thinking about the number 75. On my third attempt, I changed my focus on where I wanted to end up. I began to focus on scoring 90 points. Yes, I did work harder, but I knew that I needed to, to reach a score of 90. The next time I took the test, I was focused on scoring 90 instead of 75, and as a result, I scored an 86. While not achieving the 90, I was still able to achieve the primary goal of passing the certification.

Another example has been in running. I have had numerous goals over the years in running, and in building up to running long distances, you challenge yourself to add on a few miles (or in some cases, a few more mailboxes) to run weekly! Early in my running career, I always seemed to have a problem running a four-mile run without stopping.

I'm not really sure why but my mind just seemed to focus on that being a number I would not do well with. So instead of focusing on four miles, I went from running around three and a half miles to five miles. After several attempts of trying to get to four miles, I blew past it completely and began running five miles instead of trying to get to four miles.

So if you're trying to eat healthy once a day, lose the final five pounds, pass the exam, attend church once a month, make one more sale, make one more friend this month, go on one vacation this year, hike one more mile, read one more chapter and seem to have trouble reaching these goals, simply overshoot the primary goal by making another goal to overshoot it! Overshoot your goal, and you will be sure to reach it!

Incentives

One of the fun techniques I have used in the process of achieving lifetime goals is the use of incentives. Incentives are the rewards we give ourselves once we achieve a goal. These incentives (or rewards) can be tangible or intangible, meaning you can have something to hold on to or they can be mental rewards you give yourself once you reach your objectives.

The tangible goals are the things that you may receive or even buy yourself for completing the goal. So whether you get the bonus for completing a project at work, you get a raise because you were promoted, you buy the new swimsuit because you lost twenty pounds, you receive a trophy because you won the tournament, you win the trip because you met the sales quota, or you have a pizza party because of the success of the soccer team's or PTA's fund-raiser, whatever you can think of as a reward that can help you reach your goal can be a fun way to celebrate the success of achieving your goals.

As you have been thinking about your goal or goals, what incentives can you think of now that could help you want to complete your goals?

The intangibles can be as meaningful and even more meaningful if you carefully think them out in advance. To allow yourself a sense of peace after a long, successful struggle of battling cancer, to experience joy upon marrying after months of stress from planning and preparing for your wedding, to feel compassion after helping a local charity raise funds for those in need, or to allow one week of mental relaxation and not studying after you complete midterms can be examples of intangible incentives. While peace, joy, compassion, and relaxation weren't the goal themselves that you were trying to achieve, they can be wonderful intangible incentives to help you get through the tough times and to reach your goals.

Whether your incentives are tangible or intangible, you can enhance your chances of success with your incentives. In my profession as a human resources professional, I was leading an effort to implement a health clinic for employees. Knowing that I would become the point person for health and wellness, I decided to begin exercising. I set a goal that if I would exercise on a regular basis for several weeks, I would then buy myself a membership at the YMCA. Later having reached that goal and having joined a YMCA, I decided that if I would lose ten pounds, I would consider buying new running shoes. I reached the ten pounds after four months. Those first ten pounds were difficult as I had to increase my metabolism. Once I lost the ten pounds, I set a goal to lose ten more pounds, and then I would buy new gym shorts. Reaching this goal, I now had new shoes and new shorts, so each time I would exercise I was feeling good in that I was wearing my trophies for my accomplishments (I am not a fashionable sort of guy, so the new stuff was more of a trophy than a fashion statement). Next, I needed to lose ten more pounds, and once I did, I would go skydiving! The skydiving opportunity will require me to remain fit and, under a certain amount of weight, to remain eligible to jump.

So while I had the initial goal of remaining fit and continuing to focus on my health, I was also incentivizing myself to accomplish subgoals too while I was reaching my primary goals. Increase your success by creating incentives and have fun achieving your goals too!

Success Brings Success

One of the aspects that I have noticed in studying human behavior is that success or positive behavior can lead to more success and bad or negative behavior can lead to the lack of success and more bad behavior.

I believe it is important to set goals early in life and learn the process of achievement. To fully gain the benefit of this achievement technique, you should think about the goals that you're setting and how they can lead to other goals that you would like to accomplish in life.

So let's look at some examples of how success in some goals will lead to success in other goals.

I decided in my late teens that I enjoyed politics (actually, I knew this by age twelve but was too young to get involved). I also knew that I wanted to pursue a career in human resources. So I thought if I could get active in the student's government at my college, I would learn about politics and gain a better understanding of people in the process. I studied politics in college, started a political club on campus, ran for and was elected as student body president representing approximately twelve thousand students. Along with this, I attended every possible political campaign training event that was held either in my community or in the state. This knowledge and experience provided me with credentials that ultimately helped in being selected as congressional intern in Washington, DC. While gaining an understanding of politics and people, I would then stay active in politics while I completed an MS in psychology. By gaining a psychology degree, I learned even more about people's behavior. That helped me to be more successful in human resources. Knowing why people react the way they do also helped me further in politics.

So by going to college, I reached the initial goal of making it to college (first goal [g1]). College offered me an opportunity to pursue politics (g2) in college and kept me learning about people and leadership, which then allowed me to continue my pursuit of a human resources degree. While pursuing my degree as well as getting active with college politics, I ran for and became student body president (g3). As I completed my undergraduate degree in personnel (g4), I was able to get hired into the field of human resources (g5) and a job that paid for me to pursue an MS in psychology degree (g6), which led to me completing my degree (g7). Ultimately, the MS in psychology degree led to a better job (g8), which increased my compensation (g9). By having a more successful job and a higher compensation, I was able to pursue running for and being elected to public office (g10).

Other examples may include the following, but what do you think happens next as success brings on more success?

- As you meet your mate (g1), he or she influences you to attend church (g2) . . . leading you to? (g3).
- After losing twenty-five pounds (g1), you are able to stop taking blood pressure medication (g2) . . . allowing you to? (g3).
- By attending your first AA meeting (g1), you gain hope to stop drinking (g2) and meet others that help you to achieve your goal (g3) . . . that allow you to? (g4).
- By eliminating your addiction (g1), you save your marriage (g2). Then decide to start a family (g3) . . . allowing you as a family to? (g4).
- By reading a book on living life abundantly (g1), you are able to set a goal to? (g2).

Obviously, the concept is simple but can be extremely rewarding if you continue to think about balancing your goals in life. Having all your success in your career (or only one of the goal categories) can leave the rest of your family or your life empty.

Allow the goal-achieving process to bring success to you and then allow your success in achieving your goals to lead to even more success in other areas of life.

Multiple-Goal Setting

Sometimes pursuing one goal, particularly if it lasts several years, can be a bit daunting, and maintaining momentum and the enthusiasm to complete the goal may decrease over time. One way to overcome this diminishing enthusiasm is to create some goals that align with other goals. Instead of going after one goal, try three or four at a time! Don't become obsessive by doing too many at a time, although it can become an exciting challenge in itself to try to accomplish many goals simultaneously.

Let's begin first with two goals. Let's say that we know that we want to increase our pay and change careers. Okay, that's an easy one. We simply find a new job in the field we want to pursue.

Now let's try three goals. First, your financial goal is to increase your income, your career goal is to work in the field of medicine, and you've always wanted to travel to the northwest portion of the United States, so you pursue a degree and/or job in a hospital in Seattle.

Other examples might include that you know that you want to improve your health, spend more time with your family, find more time to spend outdoors, learn about trees in your part of the country, and visit all the state parks in your state! It becomes obvious how this works, right? Create a goal that links these individual goals together. Along with you learning about the state parks and trees, you've now educated your kids on forestry and helped them stay healthy too!

One of the goals that I've heard of included those goals from individuals that wanted to run marathons in every state in the United States. Wow, gaining an understanding of every state by visiting them while you're keeping healthy and running marathons—not a bad lineup!

If your goals include reading more, wanting a degree, becoming more social, leading a mission project, and giving back to your community, you may consider going to a Bible college! Okay, that's possibly a bit much, but you get the idea. Simply think about the various goals that you have in life and remember to maintain a balance of the variety of goals that you've set.

A particular fun exercise is to figure out how you can link several annual and/or lifetime goals together at the beginning of the year.

Teaming Up for Success

Sometimes when trying to achieve a goal, we find that we may be lacking the skills or knowledge to complete the goal alone. Or we may find that for whatever reason, we need someone else to be there to encourage or motivate us to reach our goals. This is when the technique of teaming up for success needs to be used.

Sometimes we feel that we need to accomplish our goals alone. There may be reasons that this is important, and a decision must be made if you can accomplish this goal alone. If you can reach the goal by gaining new skills, knowledge, or becoming more physically fit and completing the goal in a certain time frame, isn't a concern, than take the additional time and effort to achieve the goal on your own. It may be that you want to overcome this hurdle or to reach an objective, and you also want to look back in life and know that you achieved this one on your own.

On the other hand, teaming up with someone can be fun, exciting, and a wonderful memory that you can share with others. If completing a goal can be inspiring for you and give you a sense of pride and achievement, think how this could be shared with someone! Having someone else by your side as you finish the race can be extremely fulfilling as you get to share the excitement with someone and gain a memory for a lifetime.

Some examples that come to mind could include the following: You're single and want to eat at several of the various restaurants in your town. You're older but want to take hikes in the community parks. You're wanting to run in the morning but you are not a morning person and find it hard to wake up. You're wanting to start your own business but are not sure how. You're needing to pass trigonometry but need a tutor. You're wanting to study the Bible but would rather do it with a group. You're wanting to invest your portfolio differently but not sure where or how. You're wanting to travel overseas but scared to go alone. Or you want to learn a new language but need a trainer. These are a few examples of how you could team up with others to accomplish your goals.

A cautionary note on selecting someone to team up with, however, should be mentioned. Remember to select someone that will help you get there! Sometimes if not careful, you can select someone that may actually derail your chances, or possibly the person comes up with reasons of how your goal cannot be accomplished. So select carefully and make sure that they are as committed as you are in reaching your goals.

The Life Planners, Inc. Coach Connection

Sometimes selecting an actual coach is the best way to reach your goals! This obviously is easy to apply in the world of sports, but this technique can also be used when you're attempting to complete any specific goal too. From acting, singing, athletics, finances, religion, and/or health you can find coaches and even life coaches in nearly every area that you can imagine. They can be very effective in achieving your goals.

If you know that there is a goal that you want to achieve but are not sure of the steps you might need to consider or you have some tendencies that seem to delay or derail your progress, you may want to have a life coach assist you in achieving your goals.

An LPI certified coach can ask a variety of questions in order to better evaluate how to help you to achieve your goals. If you find that a goal is too mentally challenging or if you simply need to share the trials and tribulations with someone, an LPI coach may be someone that you can speak with in a confidential manner while discussing the pursuit objectively. Sometimes you can perceive a process, step, or way to accomplish a goal with only one possible way to reach it. A coach can provide a different perspective and provide a breakthrough idea that allows you to obtain the goal by coming at it in a totally different way.

One way that the coach can assist you is to help identify techniques that you can incent yourself. By suggesting ways to motivate you or by discussing alternatives to the path you've chosen to accomplish your goal, the coach can become a sounding board for you to mentally create ways to complete your goal.

Consider a coach for assistance in accomplishing your lifetime goals. If you need assistance in achieving your goals, consider an LPI certified coach at www.Lifeplannersnow.com.

Chapter 8
Achievement – Achieve it!

- ✓ *Overshoot It!*
  Sometimes in pursuing goals, we get hung up in the final steps to reach our goals. It could be a mental block, or even sometimes we can be worried about succeeding, or we don't have the confidence to push through to the completion of an objective. In order to beat the goal, you can actually set a new goal to exceed the original goal.

- ✓ *Incentives!*
  Having a plan to reward yourself when you accomplish either sub-goals or milestones or even when you complete the overall goal can make goal achievement fun! Incentives can be tangible or intangible rewards for achieving your goals.

- ✓ *Success Brings Success*
  By learning that being successful in achieving goals can lead to achieving more goals and thereby being more successful, you can create a pattern of success for years to come.

- ✓ *Multiple-Goal Setting*
  Setting several goals at once becomes fun and can overcome a feeling of stagnation while trying to achieve a long-term goal.

- ✓ *Team up for Success*
  When attempting to reach a lifetime goal or goals that require skills, education or experience that you may not have, you can team up with others to enjoy the success together.

- ✓ *The LPI Coach Connection*
  If you're not sure how to achieve a goal or you need assistance in strategy to reach a goal, contacting a Life Planners, Inc. Coach can provide you someone that will help to guide and inspire you toward success.

Chapter 9

PLANTING SEEDS FOR LIFETIME ACHIEVEMENT

Now that you have learned twenty-five steps on achieving your goals, what kind of goals do you want to achieve for a lifetime? As goal achievement becomes within reach, you should begin to think about making sure that you have balance in the various goals that you set in life. You should also make sure that your goals lead you to a life of abundance!

Teaching Others

A life of abundance will happen when you begin or continue to help others achieve what they want to achieve! By using the twenty-five steps of goal-achievement techniques, you can plant seeds of achievement at all stages of your life and teach others to do the same.

Most of us have obviously used one or several of the twenty-five techniques of goal achievement in our lives. However, have you used all of them? If you're struggling to accomplish a goal or several goals, try incorporating some or all the steps, and you will be amazed at how they work. I have over a lifetime of goal-setting exercises and life challenges and have found that they have worked for me and others amazingly well.

By now, you've identified several goals that you have recently thought of or remembered or pondered over the years that you've wanted to achieve. By determining which stage your goal is in, whether it's the planning and mental, action, persistence, or the achieving stage, identify the steps that you can use to move to the next step or stage. As you continue to use these techniques, they will become instinctual, and you will begin to think through these steps as you pursue any new goal. Then in the future, you'll know that you must take steps to move toward your goals. You'll know that you need to measure your goal as well as to remember that there will be roadblocks in life that will try to prevent you from achieving your goals. Ultimately, you can learn the 25-techniques of goal achievement and these simple steps will help you in reaching your goals in life.

Teaching Your Family the Steps

One of the most successful skills as a leader, parent, spouse, or friend that you can teach to others is how to achieve goals. I encourage you to pass on these techniques that you've learned either one at a time or through the use of this book so that others can learn them too. Teaching family members can be most rewarding but challenging too!

One of the first steps in teaching members of a family to set goals is to create some simple goals and processes for recording them. You might start with goals for the family, including plans for time together, vacations, activities that you might want to accomplish together. If you do this on an annual basis, it can set the tone for what the family wants to tackle in the coming year. I've encouraged my children to consider their new year's goals during the break in school around Christmas. The time when most of the world is creating New Year's resolutions (these are wishes as most of the time they are not written down, and no plans to accomplish them are made) is a great time to explain and teach the family to differentiate between a goal and a New Year's resolution. By writing goals down and discussing them as a family (those that you can share at this stage), you can gain a perspective to what your children see as important in their lives. You can also adopt some of their goals to become your family goals too. If your daughter wants to join the tennis team in the next year of school, you can create family events that include playing tennis together.

By discussing how your son or daughter is going to save $20 a month and put it into his or her savings account, you can become part of his or her goal-setting and goal-achieving process. This can be a life-learning event at a very young age that you can teach your children. Remember, if they can see it, they can achieve it!

Balance in the goals that you set in the goal-setting process is important for all ages in your family. By helping your children to first learn to pray about their goals and make sure that they keep balance in their various goals in life, at an early age, you will be teaching them an important life lesson.

Teaching teenagers this process, like many other processes, can be challenging but not impossible. In helping a teenager with goals, I would place less emphasis on lifetime goals (if they aren't sure what goals to set) and rather focus on annual and monthly goals. Most teens know what classes they will either choose or be required to take next year. They also know what current interests, hobbies, friendships, or extracurricular activities—from sports teams, band, Boy Scouts or Girl Scouts, part-time job, performing arts, even owning or beating the newest video game, to name only a few—that they can set goals for. Having them set goals for each area of life, including family and social, they can learn many aspects of visioning for the future. It may be challenging, but it will be a life skill that can lead to an abundant life!

If you want to help to get your whole family involved in setting their goals annually, contact LPI at *www.lifeplannersnow.com* to purchase the LPI Life Achievement Planner.

Picturing it for a Lifetime of Visual Memories

Today, now more than ever, you can record your accomplishments and your goals visually too. By capturing your visual memories of pursuing a goal or accomplishing a goal, you've created a picture that can last generations! So with the iPads, iPhones, Androids, digital cameras, or even regular cameras, you can take pictures while you're working out, writing your book, hiking, boating, painting, traveling, or whatever and wherever the goal can take you. Take a camera and grab a picture and take good ones because they'll last a lifetime and even longer!

This is why at Life Planners Inc. we put picture inserts into our Life Achievement Planners so that you can capture these memories and share them along with your lifetime achievements! (Life Achievement Planners are available at *www.lifeplannersnow.com*.)

After You Reach Your Goals

As a goal achiever, I've found many times in life, after planning and ultimately achieving hundreds of goals of all sizes, that it can be a bit of a letdown once you've realized that you've now reached the summit or finished the race or completed your goal. Once the excitement of achievement has been accomplished, you're now trying to assess what to do next.

So if after you got the job, completed the mission project, started eating healthy, joined the gym, completed the cooking class, learned Spanish, attended the big league baseball game, created a Facebook page, received the certification, paid off the student loans, established the 401(k) account, took a hike at the neighborhood park, learned to play lacrosse, learned sign language, planted your own garden, completed a hot-air balloon ride, learned how to laugh more, visited all the states in the United States, started your business, retired after a successful career, became single after the death of a spouse after thirty years of marriage, watched your children move out on their own, or completed reading the Bible, what happens next? If you're not sure, I recommend three options: enjoy the moment, wait, and then dream bigger!

As a goal achiever, sometimes we cannot wait until we identify new goals and immediately begin to achieve something new. However, there is wisdom in learning to be content too! Make sure that you're stopping and giving yourself an opportunity to fully appreciate your achievement and your success as well as to properly thank and give credit to those in life that have helped you to reach your goals. This process of thanking those that helped should be part of your goal-achieving journey! This step can be extremely meaningful and provide a sense of what is really important in achieving your goal. Be sure, first of all, to thank God for the goal and his guidance in accomplishing it. Take time to enjoy the moment!

Another post-achievement step beyond enjoying the moment is to simply wait and allow some time to elapse before you begin another pursuit. This waiting will possibly provide a different perspective in going forward, allow you to better process your recent achievement, and allow you to rejuvenate your enthusiasm toward your next goal. During this time, you might even be able to rethink and reevaluate goals that are important to you. You may decide a goal that you've always wanted to pursue now simply isn't a vision for your future any longer. Above all, enjoy your accomplishment because you deserve it!

After time has passed and you've allowed time to fully appreciate your accomplishment as well as celebrated your achievement, it's time to set the course for your next goal to be achieved.

To decide what goal to achieve, review your lifetime goals, assess the stage and age of your life, determine how by achieving the next goal, you can help others and above all, ask God for guidance in selecting your next goal. Don't miss the chance to learn more, help others, make an impact and to live life abundantly.

Chapter 9
Planting Seeds for Lifetime Achievement!

✓ *Teaching Others*
By learning the four stages of goal achievement and the 25 techniques to achieve your goals, you can then truly live a life of abundance by helping others learn them too.

✓ *Teaching Your Family the Steps*
Teaching children and family members the techniques of goal-achievement can lead to some great family traditions and develop skills for their lifetime.

✓ *Picture it for a lifetime of visual memories!*
Taking pictures throughout the process of setting and achieving lifetime goals can lead to capturing some amazing lifetime memories too.

✓ *After You Reach Your Goals*
What do you do once you reach your goals? Enjoy the moment, wait and then dream bigger!

Conclusion

It gives me great pleasure to have shared some of the goals of my life, but even more importantly, I hope to have sparked you in remembering your lifetime goals or allowed you an opportunity to have even dreamed a few more!

Life is about goal setting, from the pyramids, the creations of countries, the seven wonders of the world to identifying what you're going to do with the rest of your life. Goals are to be set in all stages of life, all ages of life, all socioeconomic levels, all languages, and all parts of the world. How exciting! Just think, the one thing that you have in common with every person and leader in the history of time is that they too had dreams and goals in their days just as you now have all these years later! Just as goals were identified, set, and accomplished two thousand years ago by people of all ages, this year, this month, and right now, you have the ability to dream great dreams and set goals just as they did. If success in life is based on the idea of making good decisions, goals can help to guide us in making great decisions in our lives.

By having dreams that lead to goals, you can live a life of abundance. A life of abundance can be obtained, I believe, by creating God-driven dreams. By including God in your goals in life, you're bound to dream big (I believe God wants you to), and through these goals, you will increase both faith and hope in your life. Faith and hope can add to life's excitement, adventure, success, contentment, and fulfillment, but it may also bring challenge, disappointment, disaster, and crisis at all ages and stages too. Through it all, your goals can lead you and pull you through those tough times in life as well.

The first step in the process of goal setting is to determine what dreams you have in your life, and these can be identified by needs, wants, and desires. Once you evaluate your dreams and then write them down, they become goals.

By determining what stage your goals are in, whether it's the planning and mental stage, the action stage, the persistence stage, or the achievement stage, you know that you'll need to take steps to keep your goal on a path to completion.

Once you've determined which stage the goal is in, you should then identify the specific goal-achieving techniques that will help you achieve your goal. These individual steps are best applied when all the goal-achieving techniques of the stage are used. Although even using some of the steps in each stage can help to catapult you toward achieving your goal. Take advantage of each step and think of how it relates to your goal.

After you have completed the individual goal, remember to pause and enjoy the moment of achievement! It is through this moment of accomplishment that your success can lead you to more success in life. By realizing that you can even teach this goal-achieving process to others, including your family, you can help others achieve a life of abundance too.

In a hymn called "The Hymn of Promise," we find the words that, while simple, can connect us to the heart of dreaming God-driven dreams. It's been said that only God knows the apples in a seed. Friend, only God knows the dreams you will reach in your life as the hymn points out. May you continue to plant seeds for a lifetime of achievement!

> In the bulb there is a flower; in the seed, an apple tree;
> In cocoons, a hidden promise: butterflies will soon be free!
> In the cold and snow of winter there's a spring that waits to be,
> Unrevealed until its season, something God alone can see.
>
> There's a song in every silence, seeking word and melody;
> There's a dawn in every darkness, bringing hope to you and me.
> From the past will come the future; what it holds, a mystery,
> Unrevealed until its season, something God alone can see.
>
> In our end is our beginning; in our time, infinity;
> In our doubt there is believing; in our life, eternity,
> In our death, a resurrection; at the last, a victory,
> Unrevealed until its season, something God alone can see.
>
> Natalie A. Sleeth

© 1986 Hope Publishing Company, Carol Stream, Ill. All rights reserved. Used by permission

My belief is that goals are the essence of life. Everyone needs goals to guide and direct them throughout all ages and stages of their life. Obviously, your vision for your life may change many times throughout your life, but you can begin by understanding the vision for yourself today. It may change tomorrow, and when it does, so can your goals. In the meantime, you can experience a life that is fulfilling and meaningful today through the goals that you set for yourself.

Just as in the bulb, seed or cocoon, we may never fully know what may come from first identifying, then pursuing and finally achieving the goals that are God driven. But in our pursuit we will, I believe, accomplish at least one goal for God. We know the goal by the words from Jesus when he said, as John 10:10 puts it, "I have come that you may have life and you may have it more abundantly."

I hope that you take advantage of this book by setting goals in all aspects of your life and that your spiritual goals may lead the way. Through our faith we can achieve great dreams even with adversity along the way. My hope is that you grow deeper in your faith, clearer to your life's purpose, rise up with strength and confidence to life's adversities and through it all, *Live Life Abundantly!*

Completed a lifetime goal to go skydiving on May 27, 2012.
A lifetime goal has now become a lifetime memory!

About the Author
Thomas A. Harris, MS, SPHR, CCP, CBP, GRP, CLRP

His career has included over twenty years as a human resources professional. He has served as a personnel specialist, labor relations administrator, senior consultant, manager, and director of human resource functions in various companies in and around the Fort Wayne, Indiana, community. In these roles, he has had responsibilities of assisting and leading over five thousand employees. These responsibilities have included personal counseling, training and development, and serving as a change agent for numerous organizations and employees. He has helped employees at all levels of organizations identify career and personal goals while pursuing fulfillment in their present careers. He has also served as an associate faculty member at the IPFW Department of Organizational Leadership and Supervision.

Upon his high school graduation from Northrop High in 1979, he attended IPFW, pursuing an associate's degree in supervision and later receiving a BS in personnel from Purdue University at Fort Wayne. In 1995, he received an MS in psychology from the University of Saint Francis, where he is pursuing an MBA.

He served as student body president of IPFW and president of the IPFW alumni association. He was a Fort Wayne Jaycees member, a Leadership Fort Wayne graduate, and the president of the Leadership Fort Wayne Alumni Association. He was a tutor and board member for the Three Rivers Literacy Alliance. He was an Early Bird Toastmasters club member, a lay leader and board member of Bethel United Methodist Church, a board member of Saint Joseph United Methodist Church, the chairman of the Indiana Young Republicans, a treasurer of the Boy Scout Troop 307, and board member for Huntington County United Way. He was also elected as an advisory board member for Saint Joseph Township in Allen County, Indiana. In 2010, he was elected as a county council member on the Allen County Council, representing the Second District of approximately 90,000 citizens and over 350,000 citizens of Allen County, Indiana.

His accomplishments and awards have included the following: Graduate of the Center for Creative Leadership, Colorado Springs, Colorado; certified as a senior professional of human resources (SPHR); certified compensation professional (CCP); certified benefits professional (CBP); global remuneration professional (GRP); certified labor relations professional (CLRP); certified lay speaker for the United Methodist Church; IPFW Alumni Distinguished Service awardee; Outstanding Young Men of America awardee; Indiana real estate licensee; certified competent Toastmaster; rookie legislator of the year for the Indiana Jaycees; intern for Congressman Dan Coats, Washington, DC; Who's Who Among American Colleges and Universities member; IPFW Student Leadership awardee; Certificate of Commendation awardee from the Center for the Study of the Presidency, Washington, DC; senior speaker at the graduation for Northrop High School in 1979.

He is a proud husband of twenty-seven years and father of three children, who are graduates of IPFW, Indiana University, and one who is presently attending Northrop High School. His philosophy in life is balanced between his spiritual beliefs, psychological training, and personal experience in working and serving people of all ages and stages of life.

As president and founder of Life Planners Inc. and executive director and founder of Life Planning Partners Inc., he stays active in communicating the importance of living life to the fullest through identifying and setting meaningful goals. Both organizations were founded in 2002 and continue to grow, assisting individuals of all ages in the Fort Wayne area and recently expanded to services throughout Indiana. While dedicated toward the premise that the unexamined life is not worth living, he is committed to helping people of all ages create goals that bring passion, excitement, and adventure in order for them to live life abundantly!

Appendix

Dream Sheets
Goal Sheets
Lifetime Achievement Chart
Annual Achievement Chart
Monthly Achievement Chart

Spiritual Dream Sheet

Physical and Mental Health Dream Sheet

Education Dream Sheet

Family and Social Dream Sheet

Career Dream Sheet

Financial Dream Sheet

Adventure: Exploration
Dream Sheet

Adventure: Sports/Art
Dream Sheet

Adventure: Learning
Dream Sheet

Adventure: Experiencing Dream Sheet

Spiritual Goals Sheet

Priority Code	List Goal	Possible Challenges and Roadblocks	Things I Must Do to Achieve This Goal	Start Date	Achievement Date
☐ Life ☐ 20yr ☐ 10yr ☐ 5 yr ☐ 2 yr ☐ 1 yr	Goal: Achievement Date_____	1. 2. 3. 4. 5.	1. 2. 3. 4. 5.		
☐ Life ☐ 20yr ☐ 10yr ☐ 5 yr ☐ 2 yr ☐ 1 yr	Goal: Achievement Date_____	1. 2. 3. 4. 5.	1. 2. 3. 4. 5.		
☐ Life ☐ 20yr ☐ 10yr ☐ 5 yr ☐ 2 yr ☐ 1 yr	Goal: Achievement Date_____	1. 2. 3. 4. 5.	1. 2. 3. 4. 5.		

Physical and Mental Health Goals Sheet

Priority Code	List Goal	Possible Challenges and Roadblocks	Things I Must Do to Achieve This Goal	Start Date	Achievement Date
☐ Life ☐ 20yr ☐ 10yr ☐ 5 yr ☐ 2 yr ☐ 1 yr	Goal: Achievement Date____	1. 2. 3. 4. 5.	1. 2. 3. 4. 5.		
☐ Life ☐ 20yr ☐ 10yr ☐ 5 yr ☐ 2 yr ☐ 1 yr	Goal: Achievement Date____	1. 2. 3. 4. 5.	1. 2. 3. 4. 5.		
☐ Life ☐ 20yr ☐ 10yr ☐ 5 yr ☐ 2 yr ☐ 1 yr	Goal: Achievement Date____	1. 2. 3. 4. 5.	1. 2. 3. 4. 5.		

Life Planners, Inc.
LIVE LIFE ABUNDANTLY!
LPI

Education Goals Sheet

Priority Code	List Goal	Possible Challenges and Roadblocks	Things I Must Do to Achieve This Goal	Start Date	Achievement Date
☐ Life ☐ 20yr ☐ 10yr ☐ 5 yr ☐ 2 yr ☐ 1 yr	Goal: Achievement Date____	1. 2. 3. 4. 5.	1. 2. 3. 4. 5.		
☐ Life ☐ 20yr ☐ 10yr ☐ 5 yr ☐ 2 yr ☐ 1 yr	Goal: Achievement Date____	1. 2. 3. 4. 5.	1. 2. 3. 4. 5.		
☐ Life ☐ 20yr ☐ 10yr ☐ 5 yr ☐ 2 yr ☐ 1 yr	Goal: Achievement Date____	1. 2. 3. 4. 5.	1. 2. 3. 4. 5.		

Family and Social Goals Sheet

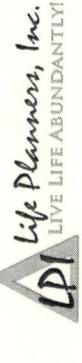
Life Planners, Inc.
LIVE LIFE ABUNDANTLY!

Priority Code	List Goal	Possible Challenges and Roadblocks	Things I Must Do to Achieve This Goal	Start Date	Achievement Date
☐ Life ☐ 20yr ☐ 10yr ☐ 5 yr ☐ 2 yr ☐ 1 yr	Goal: Achievement Date____	1. 2. 3. 4. 5.	1. 2. 3. 4. 5.		
☐ Life ☐ 20yr ☐ 10yr ☐ 5 yr ☐ 2 yr ☐ 1 yr	Goal: Achievement Date____	1. 2. 3. 4. 5.	1. 2. 3. 4. 5.		
☐ Life ☐ 20yr ☐ 10yr ☐ 5 yr ☐ 2 yr ☐ 1 yr	Goal: Achievement Date____	1. 2. 3. 4. 5.	1. 2. 3. 4. 5.		

Career Goals Sheet

Priority Code	List Goal	Possible Challenges and Roadblocks	Things I Must Do to Achieve This Goal	Start Date	Achievement Date
☐ Life ☐ 20yr ☐ 10yr ☐ 5 yr ☐ 2 yr ☐ 1 yr	Goal: Achievement Date____	1. 2. 3. 4. 5.	1. 2. 3. 4. 5.		
☐ Life ☐ 20yr ☐ 10yr ☐ 5 yr ☐ 2 yr ☐ 1 yr	Goal: Achievement Date____	1. 2. 3. 4. 5.	1. 2. 3. 4. 5.		
☐ Life ☐ 20yr ☐ 10yr ☐ 5 yr ☐ 2 yr ☐ 1 yr	Goal: Achievement Date____	1. 2. 3. 4. 5.	1. 2. 3. 4. 5.		

Financial Goals Sheet

Life Planners, Inc.
LPI — LIVE LIFE ABUNDANTLY!

Priority Code	List Goal	Possible Challenges and Roadblocks	Things I Must Do to Achieve This Goal	Start Date	Achievement Date
☐ Life ☐ 20yr ☐ 10yr ☐ 5 yr ☐ 2 yr ☐ 1 yr	Goal: Achievement Date____	1. 2. 3. 4. 5.	1. 2. 3. 4. 5.		
☐ Life ☐ 20yr ☐ 10yr ☐ 5 yr ☐ 2 yr ☐ 1 yr	Goal: Achievement Date____	1. 2. 3. 4. 5.	1. 2. 3. 4. 5.		
☐ Life ☐ 20yr ☐ 10yr ☐ 5 yr ☐ 2 yr ☐ 1 yr	Goal: Achievement Date____	1. 2. 3. 4. 5.	1. 2. 3. 4. 5.		

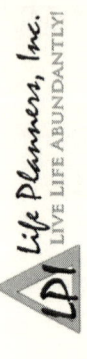

Adventure: Exploration Goals Sheet

Priority Code	List Goal	Possible Challenges and Roadblocks	Things I Must Do to Achieve This Goal	Start Date	Achievement Date
☐ Life ☐ 20yr ☐ 10yr ☐ 5 yr ☐ 2 yr ☐ 1 yr	Goal: Achievement Date____	1. 2. 3. 4. 5.	1. 2. 3. 4. 5.		
☐ Life ☐ 20yr ☐ 10yr ☐ 5 yr ☐ 2 yr ☐ 1 yr	Goal: Achievement Date____	1. 2. 3. 4. 5.	1. 2. 3. 4. 5.		
☐ Life ☐ 20yr ☐ 10yr ☐ 5 yr ☐ 2 yr ☐ 1 yr	Goal: Achievement Date____	1. 2. 3. 4. 5.	1. 2. 3. 4. 5.		

Adventure: Sports/Art Goals Sheet

Priority Code	List Goal	Possible Challenges and Roadblocks	Things I Must Do to Achieve This Goal	Start Date	Achievement Date
☐ Life ☐ 20yr ☐ 10yr ☐ 5 yr ☐ 2 yr ☐ 1 yr	Goal: Achievement Date____	1. 2. 3. 4. 5.	1. 2. 3. 4. 5.		
☐ Life ☐ 20yr ☐ 10yr ☐ 5 yr ☐ 2 yr ☐ 1 yr	Goal: Achievement Date____	1. 2. 3. 4. 5.	1. 2. 3. 4. 5.		
☐ Life ☐ 20yr ☐ 10yr ☐ 5 yr ☐ 2 yr ☐ 1 yr	Goal: Achievement Date____	1. 2. 3. 4. 5.	1. 2. 3. 4. 5.		

Life Planners, Inc.
LIVE LIFE ABUNDANTLY!

Adventure: Learning Goals Sheet

Priority Code	List Goal	Possible Challenges and Roadblocks	Things I Must Do to Achieve This Goal	Start Date	Achievement Date
☐ Life ☐ 20yr ☐ 10yr ☐ 5 yr ☐ 2 yr ☐ 1 yr	Goal: Achievement Date____	1. 2. 3. 4. 5.	1. 2. 3. 4. 5.		
☐ Life ☐ 20yr ☐ 10yr ☐ 5 yr ☐ 2 yr ☐ 1 yr	Goal: Achievement Date____	1. 2. 3. 4. 5.	1. 2. 3. 4. 5.		
☐ Life ☐ 20yr ☐ 10yr ☐ 5 yr ☐ 2 yr ☐ 1 yr	Goal: Achievement Date____	1. 2. 3. 4. 5.	1. 2. 3. 4. 5.		

Adventure: Experiencing Goals Sheet

Life Planners, Inc. — LIVE LIFE ABUNDANTLY!

Priority Code	List Goal	Possible Challenges and Roadblocks	Things I Must Do to Achieve This Goal	Start Date	Achievement Date
☐ Life ☐ 20yr ☐ 10yr ☐ 5 yr ☐ 2 yr ☐ 1 yr	Goal: Achievement Date ____	1. 2. 3. 4. 5.	1. 2. 3. 4. 5.		
☐ Life ☐ 20yr ☐ 10yr ☐ 5 yr ☐ 2 yr ☐ 1 yr	Goal: Achievement Date ____	1. 2. 3. 4. 5.	1. 2. 3. 4. 5.		
☐ Life ☐ 20yr ☐ 10yr ☐ 5 yr ☐ 2 yr ☐ 1 yr	Goal: Achievement Date ____	1. 2. 3. 4. 5.	1. 2. 3. 4. 5.		

Lifetime Achievement Chart

Lifetime Spiritual Goals

Goals	Start Date	Date Achieved

Lifetime Physical and Mental Goals

Goals	Start Date	Date Achieved

Lifetime Educational Goals

Goals	Start Date	Date Achieved

Lifetime Family and Social Goals

Goals	Start Date	Date Achieved

Lifetime Career Goals

Goals	Start Date	Date Achieved

Lifetime Financial Goals

Goals	Start Date	Date Achieved

Lifetime Adventure Goals

Experiencing/Exploration Goals

Goals	Start Date	Date Achieved

Sports/Arts Goals

Goals	Start Date	Date Achieved

Learning Goals

Goals	Start Date	Date Achieved

Annual Achievement Chart   Annual Bible Verse _____

Annual Spiritual Goals

Goals	Start Date	Date Achieved

Annual Physical and Mental Health Goals

Goals	Start Date	Date Achieved

Annual Educational Goals

Goals	Start Date	Date Achieved

Annual Family and Social Goals

Goals	Start Date	Date Achieved

Annual Career Goals

Goals	Start Date	Date Achieved

Annual Financial Goals

Goals	Start Date	Date Achieved

Annual Adventure Goals

Experiencing/Exploration Goals

Goals	Start Date	Date Achieved

Sports/Arts Goals

Goals	Start Date	Date Achieved

Learning Goals

Goals	Start Date	Date Achieved

Monthly Achievement Chart

Monthly Spiritual Goals			Monthly Physical & Mental Health Goals			Monthly Educational Goals		
Goals	Start Date	Date Achieved	Goals	Start Date	Date Achieved	Goals	Start Date	Date Achieved

Monthly Family & Social Goals			Monthly Career Goals			Monthly Financial Goals		
Goals	Start Date	Date Achieved	Goals	Start Date	Date Achieved	Goals	Start Date	Date Achieved

Monthly Adventure Goals

Experiencing/Exploration Goals			Sports/Arts Goals			Learning Goals		
Goals	Start Date	Date Achieved	Goals	Start Date	Date Achieved	Goals	Start Date	Date Achieved

Edwards Brothers Malloy
Thorofare, NJ USA
September 12, 2012